HOW TO IMPORT A EUROPEAN CAR

CAR

THE GRAY MARKET GUIDE

HOW TO IMPORT A EUROPEAN CAR

THE GRAY MARKET GUIDE

Jean Duguay

WILLIAMSON PUBLISHING
CHARLOTTE, VERMONT 05445

DEDICATION

To my father, Mr. Romeo Duguay, who has always encouraged me and believed in me.

ACKNOWLEDGEMENTS

I would like to thank Mr. Charles M. Ulrich III for his constant help and support which have enabled me to write this book.

All photographs courtesy of Koenig of West Germany and Styling Garage of West Germany (see page 57 for complete addresses), except pages 6 and 156, courtesy of Alice S. Hall; pages 108–109, courtesy of Mr. Dick Kelly, Fairway Environmental Engineering, Inc., Torrance, California (see page 113 for complete address).

Library of Congress Cataloging in Publication Data

Duguay, Jean.
    How to import a European car.

    Bibliography: p.
    Includes index.
    1. Automobile industry and trade—Europe—Directories.
2. Automobiles, Foreign—United States—Purchasing.
I. Title.
HD9710.E82D83   1985   382'.456292'029   85-24208
ISBN 0-913589-18-7

Cover and interior design: Trezzo-Braren Studio
Typography: Villanti & Sons, Printers, Inc.
Printing: Capital City Press

Williamson Publishing Co.
Charlotte, Vermont 05445

Manufactured in the United States of America

First Printing November 1985

CONTENTS

1

THE CURRENT LEGAL GRAY MARKET

The car of your dreams, at a price you deem equitable, imported without undue hassles, completely conforming to all United States customs, taxation, EPA and DOT standards—that's the promise of *How To Import A European Car: The Gray Market Guide.* Anyone can legally import a car with a little effort, a little research, and a lot of fun. Who knows—if it's in your plans—you can even manage a trip through Europe in your newly purchased car before shipping it home—and with your vehicle savings, your trip will seem free!

This book has been written so that you can privately and personally import your car and have it delivered to the United States without your ever leaving this country. You will find this book equally helpful if you plan to order and purchase your European car, taking possession of it in Europe, driving it on your European vacation, and then

shipping it home. I have discussed all the regulations to cover your travel time (European insurance, international driver's license, registration) in detail. You will also find this book very helpful if you choose to work through a private importer. In any case, I feel it is most important that you thoroughly understand every step of the importation process, no matter how much or how little of it you decide to do yourself.

In 1980, approximately 1,500 motor vehicles needing modifications in order to conform with Department of Transportation (DOT) safety standards and Environmental Protection Agency (EPA) emissions standards were imported into the United States. In 1984, more than 45,000 such gray market cars were imported. Conservative estimates are that 70,000 automobiles are expected to be imported through the legal gray market in 1985, and many thousands more in 1986.

There are three major reasons for this dramatic increase: (1) the strong U.S. dollar; (2) a greater demand for European vehicles in the United States; (3) the excessive amounts being charged in the United States by European manufacturers and their authorized dealers. This widespread private importation of automobiles into the United States has become known as the gray market, and it is completely legal.

The term "gray market" covers all vehicles not complying with United States regulations which are imported by private parties rather than the vehicles' manufacturers. *Participation in the gray market is legal if the vehicles are modified to meet all the regulations and standards of the Department of Transportation (DOT) and the Environmental Protection Agency (EPA).*

Many authorized dealers and manufacturers have tried to stop or slow the American gray market in European cars. German manufacturers have strictly ordered their authorized dealers in Europe not to sell any vehicles to foreigners, particularly Americans. Yet, even with this restriction, Americans continue to privately import thousands of

Mercedes, BMWs, Porsches, and other makes. The state of California will not even register privately imported automobiles which have been driven fewer than 7,500 miles (which incidentally has not slowed importation done through other legal channels). Actually, California, New York, Texas, and Florida are the most popular states at this time for private importation, although the popularity is rapidly spreading throughout many other states.

Pending Legislation

There has been much written lately about the mounting pressure from European manufacturers to stop the growing United States gray market. However, at this time, it seems that these efforts will actually improve the situation for private importation. The effort in Congress concerning the gray market is now focused on addressing the complaints of those involved in importation transactions. Specifically, it seems that there will be an effort made to improve safety enforcements, to ease the way for bonding, and to clear up some of the "red tape" and excessive paper work presently involved.

The gray market continues to grow by leaps and bounds. People have become more aware of the enormous savings that result from buying an automobile in Europe, and they like the purely European look that their cars have over the "made-for-America" imports. Twenty-five percent or more may be saved by buying the vehicle abroad, and it all can be done in compliance with all DOT and EPA rules and regulations.

WHY THE CONTROVERSY?

Why all the controversy then? Well, it is a controversial subject because the general public is uninformed about the proper legal procedures necessary to bring an imported car into compliance with DOT and EPA standards. And, obviously, it is also controversial because the individuals who wish to privately import cars are not as well-organized to lobby on their own behalf (and on behalf of free enterprise) as are the wealthy major European car manufacturers who are interested in protecting their lucrative, exclusive United States dealerships.

Currently, there are two popular anti-gray-market myths I'd like to put to rest.

1. Imported vehicles are converted and tested improperly to comply with the DOT and EPA standards.

First of all, I urge you to carefully read this complete book so you will know how to follow the letter of the law and get your car modified properly. Unfortunately, in this world, there are always people who will try to charge for work that they have either not done properly or have not done at all. However, this guidebook provides you with sufficient knowledge to choose, at your convenience, from the best, most reputable, fully legal conversion centers and testing laboratories. Fortunately, the government is continually cracking down on substandard conversion centers and testing laboratories, but it is still your responsibility to choose from the reputable ones available.

2. Some people feel the generous savings through private importation is solely due to the favorable exchange rates (high value of the U.S. dollar against the European currencies).

It is true that the high value of the U.S. dollar helps to make importation profitable and attractive, but that certainly is not the only reason for savings through private importation. The fluctuation of the U.S. dollar varies greatly from week to week. It is up to you to check closely *daily* in order to know when to make your best purchase, waiting for the strongest U.S. dollar against European currencies.

But, even without the present favorable exchange rate, the main reason for importing your car is the fact that you are avoiding the distributor for North America, the local dealer, and all the expenses that they both incur in running a business (advertising, showroom, etc.). Of course, you save by avoiding all these middlemen.

Another reason for private importation is that the local dealers are on a set allocation for most European cars, so availability is an important issue. You can also, through private importation, get models that aren't available through most United States dealerships and drive a truly European car. But, equally important, the demand is higher than what the authorized local dealer can meet in a reasonable time period for a reasonable price.

ANTI~ GRAY~ MARKET MYTHS

SAVINGS TELL THE STORY

To give you an approximate idea of the great savings in purchasing a vehicle in Europe compared to the same one bought through the manufacturer's dealership in the United States, see Tables 1–1 and 1–2. Table 1–1 is a completed cost comparison which illustrates the kinds of savings you can expect. Table 1–2 is to be filled out as you negotiate your car deal and plan your importation.

I encourage you to fill out Table 1–2 as you move through the importation process, and refer to it often. That way you will have no surprises as to the overall cost of your car importation. You will also know if you are getting a good deal, and how much you want to spend on extras, as well as which optional services along the way you want to do yourself, and which you wish to buy. *As with every complex business deal, it is your responsibility to keep the costs in check.* If you do, I have no doubt that you will realize great savings and great satisfaction.

It's important that you understand your potential 25 percent savings depends on several things.

- **Your ability to find a good "deal" from a reputable dealer.**

- **Buying at the right time. This can mean waiting for a favorable exchange rate (even waiting for the exact day can mean a savings of many U.S. dollars). It can also mean waiting until the end of the model year and getting a current model instead of the newer model. Obviously, the dealer wants to sell his last year's models so prices are good, much the same as with American manufactured cars in U.S. dealerships. European models change in the September–October time period.**

- **Because the prices for shipping, conversion, bonding and taxes are about the same overall for every car, the more expensive your car is the greater the savings will be. So, for example, you will save a lot more when buying a Porsche 928S than you would on any Volkswagen model.**

$

Table 1-1

➔

• Page 12

Table 1-2

➔

• Page 13

Table 1-1

SAMPLE COST COMPARISON
U.S.-PURCHASED vs. EUROPEAN-PURCHASED

IMPORTER'S NAME AND ADDRESS:

_____

_____

MAKE AND MODEL: **Mercedes-Benz 500SEC**

MODEL YEAR: **1985**

COUNTRY OF ORIGIN: **West Germany**

OPTIONS: **Fully equipped (same as comparative U.S. model)**

EXCHANGE RATE OF THE DAY: **1 U.S. dollar = 3.10 deutsch-mark**

SERVICES	COST EXPLANATION	ACTUAL COST	COMMENTS
Shipping	Depends on vehicle size	$ 866	
Freight Forwarding Agent	About $300 U.S.	0	Was not used
Marine Insurance	About 1% of European purchase price	340	
Customs Bond	About 1% of European purchase price	340	
Customs House Broker	Depends on services	510	Handling at dock $85 Cust. clearance $175 Bonding fee $250
Customs Duty	2.6% of European purchase price	884	
State Sales Tax	Your home state sales tax	2210	California 6.5%
Conversion (DOT & EPA)	See Chapter 10	4750	DOT & EPA
Other Services	Miscellaneous	0	
Cost of Car Purchased in Europe		34000	International plates, insurance
Total Cost (Delivered to your door)		43900	
Cost of Car Purchased in United States		58000	
Total Savings (U.S. purchase price minus total delivered cost)		14100	

Table 1-1.   _This typical transaction resulted in an approximate savings of 25 percent over the United States market price._

Table 1-2

YOUR IMPORTATION COST RECORD

U.S.-PURCHASED vs. EUROPEAN-PURCHASED

IMPORTER'S NAME AND ADDRESS:

_____

_____

MAKE AND MODEL: _____

MODEL YEAR: _____

COUNTRY OF ORIGIN: _____

OPTIONS: _____

EXCHANGE RATE OF THE DAY: _____

SERVICES	COST EXPLANATION	ACTUAL COST	COMMENTS
Shipping	Depends on vehicle size		
Freight Forwarding Agent	About $300 U.S.		
Marine Insurance	About 1% of European purchase price		
Customs Bond	About 1% of European purchase price		
Customs House Broker	Depends on services		
Customs Duty	1985: 2.6 percent 1986: 2.5 percent		
State Sales Tax	Your home state sales tax		
Conversion (DOT & EPA)	Your actual fee		
Other Services	Miscellaneous		
Cost of Car Purchased in Europe			
Total Cost (Delivered to your door)			
Cost of Car Purchased in United States			
Total Savings (U.S. purchase price minus total delivered price)			

Table 1-2. *By keeping careful track of all costs, you can achieve a significant savings even when hiring reliable companies and brokers to help in your importation.*

AVOID
NEWSPAPER
ADS

Be Informed!

Of course, a major stumbling block faced by many people who would like to import their own car is the complexity — or what they perceive as the complexity — in buying a car abroad, shipping it to the United States, and converting the car to meet American safety and emission standards. Up to now there has been no reliable source to whom these people could turn for accurate information.

How To Import A European Car takes all the uncertainty out of the process. The addresses provided here are reliable at the time of this printing (ownership and management changes impact on reliability so always doublecheck all references — even those listed herein). You may also turn to friends who have *successfully* imported cars for verification on these and other *proven* sources. But do avoid, at all costs, names and addresses you'll find in newspaper ads without personal verification. These are often traps for the uninitiated.

Anyone attempting to import a nonconforming vehicle for the first time without a reliable guide will be faced with many problems and many questions to which he cannot easily find answers. These problems arise primarily because American buyers and European dealers know very little if anything about United States importation regulations and strict United States safety and emission standards.

Your automobile represents a sizable investment. Great care should be taken in selecting a reliable conversion center. This guide will help you do that. In the past, modifiers were not easy to find. Now they are easier to find, but they are not all qualified. Their work will not only have to satisfy you; it will have to pass tests and inspections by the Department of Transportation and the Environmental Protection Agency.

Importing a vehicle into the United States without understanding all the details could turn out to be an expensive nightmare. However, reading this guide will help you to understand all those details. If at first glance, the task of importing your own car seems terribly complicated and time-consuming, do not be intimidated. I have given you a complete overview of the process of importing, modifying, and certifying your vehicle, along with a step-by-step checklist.

Everyone should be aware of all the procedures, regulations, and laws when importing a nonconforming vehicle to his home state. In 1984 more than 500 gray market vehicles were seized by U.S. Customs for failure to meet U.S. safety and emission requirements. While this is not a high percentage, no one wants to go through that experience, disappointment, and financial loss.

The information in this book is provided to let you know everything involved in the importation and modification of a car, but this does not mean that you will have to personally handle every detail. Ninety percent of the work can be turned over to your dealer in Europe, your shipper, your customs house broker in the United States, and your converter. You need to be familiar with procedures and regulations in order to oversee the work done by your dealer, shipper, customs house broker, and converter. You need not take care of all the details yourself, but you should know what is going on.

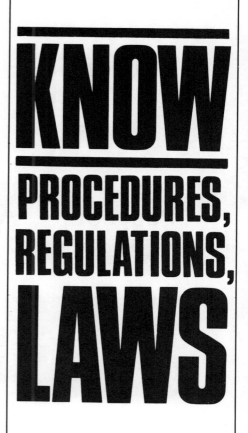

KNOW PROCEDURES, REGULATIONS, LAWS

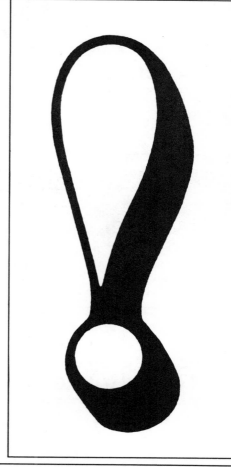

Jaguar	Lamborghini	Volkswagen
Peugeot		Saab
Mercedes		Ferrari
Renault		Porsche
Audi		Volvo
Rolls-Royce	BMW	Maserati

PART

I

PURCHASING YOUR CAR

2

FINDING THE RIGHT CAR

Automobile dealers in Europe are just like automobile dealers in the United States. Some are honest and helpful. Some are barracudas who don't want to hear from you the moment you drive the car off the lot. Be particularly careful when buying from dealers in Europe because once you have returned to the United States, it is difficult to contact them if you have any problems with your car.

The basics of buying a car in Europe are very simple. Don't rush. Be cautious and circumspect. Take the time to find the vehicle of your dreams. Stay clear of all motorcycles. If you follow these guidelines your savings can be enormous.

SOME PRECAUTIONARY MEASURES

You should be aware that a strong black market in stolen vehicles exists in Europe. European auto thieves attempt to distribute their stolen vehicles in the United States. The vehicles involved in this black market have been stolen both from private owners and from the factory. Many of these cars are discovered and seized by U.S. Customs and returned to their owners. If this should happen to you, you will of course lose everything you have spent in purchasing and shipping the car. Therefore, I strongly recommend that before you purchase a car in Europe you personally contact the FBI or Interpol to make sure the car you are interested in is not on the international listing of stolen vehicles.

Interpol now has a highly computerized system for tracking stolen cars. Be sure to insist that your dealer contacts the local police in the dealership's city and has your prospective vehicle's identification number (V.I.N.) verified as not being stolen. Have this done before you purchase your car, and ask for written verification that this has been done before paying for the car. Remember, *new cars* can be on the black market, too, because they are stolen directly from the manufacturers, so this checking should be done for new as well as used car purchases.

Most of the dealers in Europe know nothing about the Department of Transportation (DOT) and the Environmental Protection Agency (EPA) regulations. They will tell you it is perfectly OK to buy the car they are trying to sell you. After the contract is signed and the car is paid for, they will supply you with a questionable list of supposed conversion centers in your home state. The dealers in Europe don't necessarily know how reliable or competent American converters are. *Select your own converter; assume the car you are buying does not meet any of the DOT or EPA regulations.* Rely on your own judgment. Be very skeptical of Europeans who claim to know American regulations.

Be leery of any vehicles bearing DOT and EPA labels certifying that they meet those agencies' safety and emission standards. These labels are undoubtedly false. Do not buy one of these vehicles, even if the dealer gives you a written guarantee stipulating that it meets all DOT and EPA requirements. You should assume that any vehicle you purchase will have to be modified. Therefore, before buying a car make sure by checking with your modifier that it can, in fact, be easily modified.

BLACK
MARKET
CARS

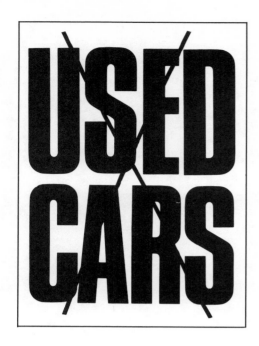

Buying Used Cars

I cannot recommend that you buy a used car, although I know many people do this. You must be aware that you are oftentimes buying another person's problems and head-aches. And, even more so than when buying a used car in the United States, you are on your own once you get it stateside.

Just as in the United States, there are some honest used car dealers, but there are also many fast-talking quick buck artists. You know the old story about the elderly grand-mother's car which was never driven at night or in the winter. Beware!

Unless you know the dealer in Europe very well or have European friends and relatives who personally know the European dealer, I'd advise that you stay away from used cars no matter how honest and tempting the offer seems.

If you must buy a used car, then set a mileage limit of 20,000 to 25,000 miles on it. Have it checked from the front bumper to the rear bumper, just as you would do in the United States. Do not be impulsive. Once you return to the United States it will be expensive and time-consuming—perhaps impossible—to correct mistakes made in haste. The best used car buys in Europe are Mercedes, BMW, and Porsche. They are by far the easiest cars to modify and to have serviced in the United States. These cars can also be purchased at a greater savings than other makes. Be aware also that some limitations exist in obtaining warranties on newly-purchased used cars.

Stay away from importing motorcycles altogether. When imported, the larger engines are subject to a 49 percent tax! More importantly, there are no longer labs to test motorcycles' emissions. Therefore, I can not recommend importing a European motorcycle under any circumstances.

Buying Independent Warranties

You should be aware that you may have some slight troubles with warranties and service in the United States. First, the American dealers will not honor the one-year, unlimited mileage guarantee for vehicles equipped with fuel injection systems. Their reason will be that a "nonauthorized" conversion center has modified your vehicle with a catalyzer. Many American authorized dealers will not accept your vehicle for service if anything has been modified. They will find some excuse to give for refusing to service your car. Needless to say, you won't receive any warranty service from them.

It may be wise to buy an independent warranty policy from a reputable American warranty company. Comprehensive warranties covering most mechanical and electrical components for periods up to six years are now available. Premiums vary according to the classification of vehicle covered, but service contracts are even available on diesel and turbo-charged engines.

To have your vehicle serviced under your warranty service contract, simply go to one of the many independent garages across the United States which specializes in servicing foreign automobiles. You will be more than welcome and the service will be just as good, if not better, than at an authorized dealership.

For complete information on warranty service contracts for your European automobile call or write:

International Warranty Corporation
5030 Camino de la Siesta
Suite 106
San Diego, California   92108

Telephone: (800) 532-4800   (Nationwide)
(800) 452-6700   (California)

Comparing United States and European Prices

Table 2–1 compares the prices of automobiles in Europe and the United States. The prices are generally valid for the 1985 and 1986 model years. Prices in the U.S. market are quoted in U.S. dollars, and prices in Europe are quoted in West German marks (as well as U.S. dollars for approximate comparisons only). Because of the continuous fluctuation of European exchange rates against the dollar compute the exact cost in dollars using the cost in West German marks and the exchange rate on the date of purchase. (The European currency used throughout this book is the West German mark.)

COMPUTING THE DOLLAR VALUE

In order to compute the dollar value of a price quoted in a European currency, first find the exact exchange rate of the day. Exchange rates are published in business or international newspapers. They are also available from your bank. Then you simply divide the European price by the exchange rate. For example, if the exchange rate of the day is

1 U.S. dollar = 3.24 West German marks (D.M.)
and
a Porsche 928S costs 86,090 D.M.
then
86,090 D.M. divided by 3.24 = 26,570 U.S. dollars

The prices in Table 2–1 may vary slightly or even considerably depending on five factors:

1. **Fluctuation of the U.S. dollar**

2. **The country in which you buy the vehicle**

3. **Your ability to "deal" with the dealer and the international rate of exchange**

4. **The availability of the vehicle**

5. **Price increases by the manufacturers**

The price lists are provided to give you an approximate price of the car you will buy and to compare the prices in the two markets. ("Not available" means the specific model is not available from authorized dealers in the United States.)

• Pages 24 to 31

Table 2-1

UNITED STATES & EUROPEAN AUTOMOBILE PRICES

1986 MODEL YEARS

MAKE & MODEL	COST IN U.S. ($)	COST IN EUROPE ($)	(DM)	hp/cc's
ALFA ROMEO				
2000 Spider Convertible	18720	8368	25941	128/1962
GTV 6 2.5 L	17680	10003	31009	158/2492
Alfa 33 1.3 L	N/A	4895	15172	75/1351
Alfa 33 1.5 L	N/A	5162	16000	84/1490
Sprint 1.3	N/A	5512	17087	85/1351
Sprint 1.5 Quadrifoglio	N/A	6104	18924	105/1490
Giulietta 1.8 L	N/A	6687	20730	122/1779
Giulietta 2.0 Turbo Diesel	N/A	7119	22071	130/1995
Alfetta 1.8	N/A	6748	20920	122/1779
Alfetta 2.4 Turbo Diesel	N/A	8356	25904	95/2393

*Notes to the price list

DM is the abbreviation for West German deutsch-mark.

NA means "not available from authorized dealers in the United States."

Horsepower **(hp)** and cubic centimeters **(cc)** information is given to aid in computing insurance costs in Chapter 7.

Cost in Europe is provided to give you an approximate idea of what the vehicles would cost in U.S. dollars in Europe, based on a 3.10 exchange rate. This value will change due to fluctuations in the exchange rate. To get a more current dollar value, divide the figure in **Cost in Europe DM** by the exchange rate of the day.

(Continued next page)

Table 2-1 (continued)

UNITED STATES & EUROPEAN AUTOMOBILE PRICES

1986 MODEL YEARS

MAKE & MODEL	COST IN U.S. ($)	COST IN EUROPE ($)	(DM)	hp/cc's
AUDI				
4000 Auto./100 Auto.	15600	7563	23445	90/1781
5000S Turbo/2005 Turbo	24960	16196	50207	182/2144
Quattro 5 Sp. Turbo Inj.	38480	21895	67874	200/2144
80 Aut.	N/A	6554	20317	75/1600
80 Diesel Aut.	N/A	6999	21697	54/1600
80 CC Aut.	N/A	7225	22400	90/1800
80 CC Diesel Aut.	N/A	7390	22909	54/1600
80 CC Turbo Diesel 5 Sp.	N/A	7597	23550	70/1600
80 CD Aut.	N/A	7867	24387	90/1800
80 CD Diesel Aut.	N/A	8031	24896	54/1600
80 CD Turbo Diesel 5 Sp.	N/A	8238	25537	70/1600
80 Quattro 5 Sp.	N/A	8707	26991	90/1800
100 Avant Aut.	N/A	10832	33579	138/2220
100 Avant Diesel Aut.	N/A	10761	33359	70/2000
100 Avant Turbo Diesel Aut.	N/A	11831	36676	87/2000
100 CC Avant Aut.	N/A	11290	34999	138/2200
100 CC Avant Diesel Aut.	N/A	11219	34778	70/2000
100 CC Avant Turbo Diesel Aut.	N/A	12288	38092	87/2000
100 CD Avant Aut.	N/A	12752	39531	138/2200
100 CD Avant Turbo Diesel Aut.	N/A	13751	42628	87/2000
100 CC Aut.	N/A	10476	32475	138/2200
100 CC Diesel Aut.	N/A	10407	32261	70/2200
100 CC Turbo Diesel Aut.	N/A	11475	35572	87/2000
100 CD Aut.	N/A	11940	37014	138/2200
100 CD Diesel Aut.	N/A	11869	36793	70/2000
100 CD Turbo Diesel Aut.	N/A	12938	40107	87/2000
100 CS Aut.	N/A	11488	35612	138/2200
100 CS Avant Aut.	N/A	12302	38136	138/2200
200 Aut.	N/A	14250	44175	138/2200

(Continued next page)

Table 2-1 (continued)

UNITED STATES & EUROPEAN AUTOMOBILE PRICES

1986 MODEL YEARS

MAKE & MODEL	COST IN U.S. ($)	COST IN EUROPE ($)	(DM)	hp/cc's
BMW				
318i Aut.	15600	7151	22168	105/1766
325/323i Aut.	21840	9408	29164	150/2316
528i Aut.	26000	11747	36415	184/2788
735i Aut.	39520	17666	54764	218/3453
633/635csi. Aut.	44720	21666	67164	218/3453
M635	N/A	28623	88731	286/3453
316 Aut.	N/A	6846	21222	90/1766
320i Aut.	N/A	9022	27968	125/1990
745i Aut.	N/A	24370	75547	252/3430
628csi Aut.	N/A	20640	63984	184/2788
FERRARI				
308 GTSI	66560	35000	108500	240/2926
Mondial Convertible	68640	44000	136400	240/2926
400i GT Aut.	N/A	50000	155000	315/4823
Testa Rosa	N/A	82000	254200	350/5000
308 GT Berlina	N/A	36809	114107	240/2927
Mondial	N/A	40295	124914	240/2927
JAGUAR				
XJ6 Sovereign 4.2 Aut.	33000	19000	58900	205/4235
Vanden Plas 5.3 HE Aut.	37602	25132	77909	295/5345
XJS HE Aut.	38070	23380	72478	295/5345
3.4	N/A	15776	48905	119/3442
Sovereign 5.3	N/A	22542	69880	295/5345
LAMBORGHINI				
Jalpa	57200	30951	95948	255/3483
Countach LP 5000S	104000	55466	171944	375/4754
MASERATI				
2.5 L Bi-Turbo	27274	17498	54243	190/2491
Quatroporte	69160	36316	112579	280/4930

*Abbreviations:
   Aut. = Automatic
   Sp. = Speed
   OD = Overdrive

(Continued on next page)

Table 2-1 (continued)

UNITED STATES & EUROPEAN AUTOMOBILE PRICES

1986 MODEL YEARS

MAKE & MODEL	COST IN U.S. ($)	COST IN EUROPE ($)	(DM)	hp/cc's
MERCEDES-BENZ				
190	27560	9500	29450	90/1997
190 2.3 16 Valves ABS	N/A	19000	58900	185/2229
230 E	N/A	12000	37200	136/2299
300 D	33280	12500	38750	109/2498
380 SE	45760	24000	74400	218/3818
380 SEL	N/A	25000	77500	204/3839
280 SL	N/A	23000	71300	185/2746
380 SL	47840	27000	83700	218/3818
500 SL	N/A	30000	93000	240/4473
500 SEL	55120	29000	89900	240/4973
500 SEC	60000	33000	102300	240/4973
190 D	N/A	11289	34995	72/1997
190 E	N/A	12062	37392	122/1997
200 D	N/A	11489	35615	60/1988
240 D	N/A	12254	37987	72/2399
240 TD	N/A	13989	43365	72/2399
280E	N/A	15875	49212	185/2746
280 TE Wagon	N/A	17581	54501	185/2746
280 SE	N/A	19956	61863	185/2746
280 SEL	N/A	21130	65503	185/2746
230 CE	N/A	15072	46723	136/2299
280 CE	N/A	17868	55390	185/2746
380 SEL	N/A	25288	78392	204/3839
380 SEC	N/A	32032	99299	204/3839
PORSCHE				
944	26000	13288	43053	163/2479
911 Carrera Targa	43000	19650	63666	231/3164
911 Carrera Cabriolet	46000	20793	67369	231/3164
928S Aut.	50000	26571	86090	300/4664
930 Turbo	N/A	30047	97352	300/3299
924 (2.0) 5 Sp.	N/A	10773	33396	125 hp

(Continued on next page)

Table 2-1 (continued)

UNITED STATES & EUROPEAN
AUTOMOBILE PRICES

1986 MODEL YEARS

MAKE & MODEL	COST IN U.S. ($)	COST IN EUROPE ($)	(DM)	hp/cc's
PEUGEOT				
505 Sti Turbo Diesel	19968	10895	33774	80/2304
505 GTD Turbo Aut.	19968	10895	33774	80/2304
505 Station Wagon Sti Turbo	20802	10595	32844	100/1971
205 GR	N/A	4440	13764	60/1360
205 GRD	N/A	5291	16402	60/1768
305 GL · OR	N/A	5085	15763	74/1472
305 GT · OR · PS	N/A	6361	19719	94/1580
305 GRD · OR · PS	N/A	6668	20670	65/1905
305 BREAK GRD · PS	N/A	6822	21148	65/1905
505 GL 2.0 Aut.	N/A	6597	20450	96/1971
505 GLD 2.5 or Aut.	N/A	6844	21216	76/2498
505 BREAK GRD PS	N/A	9007	27921	76/2498
505 FAMILIALE GRDPS	N/A	9269	28733	76/2498
604 GTi	N/A	10343	32063	155/2849
605 GTi Aut.	N/A	10943	33923	155/2849
604 GTD Turbo	N/A	10939	33910	95/2498
604 GTD Turbo Aut.	N/A	11539	35770	95/2498
ROLLS-ROYCE				
Silver Spirit	99500	71412	231374	210/6750
Silver Spur	109000	82349	266810	210/6750
Corniche Convertible	156000	92777	300597	210/6750
Camargue	1570000	111698	361901	210/6750
Bentley Mulsanne	98500	71412	231374	210/6750
Bentley Mulsanne Turbo	108000	80460	260690	310/6750
SAAB				
900	13000			100/1985
900 Turbo	19968	9484	29400	145/1985
Turbo 16 (5 Doors)	N/A	12740	39494	N/A
Turbo 16S (3 Doors)	N/A	13078	40541	N/A
CD	N/A	15964	49488	N/A

(Continued on next page)

Table 2-1 (continued)

UNITED STATES & EUROPEAN AUTOMOBILE PRICES

1986 MODEL YEARS

MAKE & MODEL	COST IN U.S. ($)	COST IN EUROPE ($)	(DM)	hp/cc's
VOLKSWAGEN				
Jetta	10000	6673	2686	75/1595
Rabit Convertible	13500	7460	23126	112/1781
Special White Rabbit Convertible	14352	7791	24152	112/1781
Scirocco	12480	6503	20159	112/1781
Polo				
C	N/A	4100	12710	40/1050
CL	N/A	4500	13950	40/1050
Classic C 4 Sp.	N/A	4296	13317	40/1050
Classic CL 4 Sp.	N/A	4695	14554	55/1300
Coupe C 4 Sp.	N/A	4454	13807	55/1300
Coupe CL 4 Sp.	N/A	4862	15072	55/1300
Coupe GT 4 Sp.	N/A	5523	17121	75/1300
Golf				
Convertible GLi K-Jetronic Fuel Inj.	N/A	8803	27289	112/1800
C Aut.	N/A	5598	17353	75/1600
C Diesel Aut.	N/A	5888	18252	54/1600
C Turbo Diesel (4 & E Sp.)	N/A	6154	19077	70/1600
C Formel E 4 Sp.	N/A	4957	15366	55/1300
CL Aut.	N/A	5943	18423	75/1600
CL Diesel Aut.	N/A	6231	19316	54/1600
CL Turbo Diesel (4 & E Sp.)	N/A	6498	20143	70/1600
CL Formel E 4 Sp.	N/A	5300	16430	55/1300
GL Aut.	N/A	6452	20001	55/1600
GL Diesel Aut.	N/A	6740	20894	54/1600
GL Turbo Diesel (4 & E Sp.)	N/A	7007	21721	70/1600
GL Formel E 4 Sp.	N/A	5779	17914	55/1300
GTD (4 & E Sp.)	N/A	6798	21073	70/1600
GTi 5 Sp.	N/A	7378	22871	112/1800
Carat Aut.	N/A	8092	25085	90/1800

(Continued on next page)

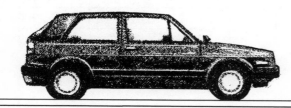

Table 2-1 (continued)

UNITED STATES & EUROPEAN AUTOMOBILE PRICES

1986 MODEL YEARS

MAKE & MODEL	COST IN U.S. ($)	COST IN EUROPE ($)	(DM)	hp/cc's
Jetta				
C Diesel Aut.	N/A	6236	19331	54/1600
C Turbo Diesel (4 & E Sp.)	N/A	6487	20109	70/1600
CL Aut.	N/A	6478	20081	90/1800
CL Diesel Aut.	N/A	6573	20376	54/1600
CL Turbo Diesel (4 & E Sp.)	N/A	6824	21154	70/1600
GL Aut.	N/A	6673	20686	75/1600
GL Diesel Aut.	N/A	6977	21628	54/1600
GL Turbo Diesel (4 & E Sp.)	N/A	7229	22409	70/1600
Carat Aut.	N/A	8405	26055	90/1800
Scirocco				
GT 5 Sp.	N/A	7654	23727	112/1800
GTL Aut.	N/A	7620	23622	112/1800
GTX 5 Sp.	N/A	8354	25897	90/1800
Passat				
C Aut.	N/A	6590	20429	90/1800
C Diesel Aut.	N/A	6850	21235	54/1600
C Turbo Diesel (4 & E Sp.)	N/A	7060	21886	70/1600
CL Aut.	N/A	6947	21535	90/1800
CL Diesel (4 & E Sp.)	N/A	6846	21222	54/1600
CL Turbo Diesel (4 & E Sp.)	N/A	7417	22992	70/1600
GL Aut.	N/A	7503	23259	90/1800
GL Diesel Aut.	N/A	7764	24068	54/1600
GL Turbo Diesel	N/A	7974	24719	70/1600
Carat Aut.	N/A	9555	29620	115/2000
C Variant Aut.	N/A	6771	20990	90/1800
C Variant Turbo Diesel (4 & E Sp.)	N/A	7241	22447	70/1600
CL Variant Aut.	N/A	7137	22124	90/1800
CL Variant Diesel Aut.	N/A	7398	22933	54/1600
CL5 Variant Aut.	N/A	8017	24852	115/2000
GL Variant Aut.	N/A	7552	23411	90/1800
GL Variant Turbo Diesel (4 & E Sp.)	N/A	8232	25519	70/1600
GL5 Variant Aut.	N/A	8641	26787	115/2000

(Continued on next page)

Table 2-1 (continued)

UNITED STATES & EUROPEAN AUTOMOBILE PRICES

1986 MODEL YEARS

MAKE & MODEL	COST IN U.S. ($)	COST IN EUROPE ($)	(DM)	hp/cc's
Santana				
CX (4 & E Sp.)	N/A	6587	20419	90/1800
CX Diesel (4 & E Sp.)	N/A	6774	20999	54/1600
CX Turbo Diesel (4 & E Sp.)	N/A	7345	22769	70/1600
LX Aut.	N/A	7266	22524	90/1800
LX Diesel Aut.	N/A	7519	23308	54/1600
LX Turbo Diesel (4 & E Sp.)	N/A	7660	23746	70/1600
LX5 Aut.	N/A	8135	25218	115/2000
GX Aut.	N/A	8236	25531	90/1800
GX Diesel Aut.	N/A	8489	26315	90/1800
GX Turbo Diesel (4 & E Sp.)	N/A	8630	26753	70/1600
GX5 Aut.	N/A	9111	28244	115/2000
GX Formel (4 & E Sp.)	N/A	7924	24564	90/1800
VOLVO				
740GL Open Roof; Aut.; OD	15600	8627	26743	114/2313
760GLE Turbo Diesel Aut.	25480	14173	43936	109/2383
240 DL 4 Sp. Sedan	N/A	6773	20996	
240 GL 5 Sp. Station Wagon	N/A	8359	25912	N/A
240 Diesel Sp. & OD Station Wagon	N/A	9685	30023	N/A
240 GLT Sp. & OD Sedan	N/A	8905	27605	N/A
245 Turbo Sp. & OD Station Wagon	N/A	10634	32965	N/A
740 GLE Aut. & OD	N/A	11037	34214	N/A
760 GLE Aut. & OD	N/A	14885	46143	N/A
760 Turbo Sp. & OD	N/A	15405	47755	N/A

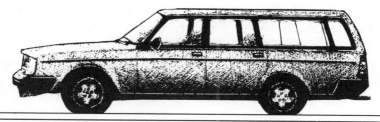

Where to Buy: Reputable Dealers

Since dealing with a reputable dealer is key to a successful importation, I've listed some of the major reliable and reputable dealers in Europe. They are used to dealing with Americans, and most of them are aware that there are strict United States regulations which the car they sell you will have to meet. They should offer you full service: registration, insurance and shipping.

I recommend that you do your "shopping" in Belgium, Germany and perhaps the Netherlands. You will find some very good bargains in these countries, and their dealers are accustomed to working with American buyers. Also, while the black market exists in these countries, it is held in check much more than in other European countries, so you can feel more secure in your purchase. Since these countries are all close together, it will be easy enough for you to shop in all three countries before making your final decision, if you are buying your car while in Europe.

Mercedes, Porsche, and BMW have strictly ordered their dealerships in Germany to stop selling vehicles to foreigners, especially Americans. They are trying to clamp down on the fast-growing American automotive gray market which is taking business away from their American dealers. The way to get around this rather minor obstacle is to buy from a small, reputable independent European automobile dealer.

If you choose to buy from dealers not listed in this book, then at the very least, try to personally contact someone who has bought through the dealer of your choice. The dealers listed here are the ones I personally know. Of course, there are others who are honest and reputable, but you must rely on your own feelings and your experience in negotiating with people. If you have never heard of a dealer before, and can find no reliable verification as to honesty and ability to fulfill on an agreement, then I'd advise you to pass up the dealership. This is nothing more than being streetwise.

And remember to confirm what you expect in a "full service" agreement: registration, titling documents, international transit plates and refunds of duty. Also, you want assistance on insurance including car insurance while driving in Europe. For shipping, you should expect marine insurance, steam cleaning, shipping arrangements including bringing your vehicle to the port of deportation. These are normal services. If your dealer is unwilling to fulfill on these, then seriously consider buying elsewhere.

Dealerships

Transco SA
Noordelaan   95
B-2030 Antwerp
Belgium

Telephone: 03-542-62-40
Telex: 35-207   Trans B

Specialties: Alfa Romeo, Audi, BMW, Jaguar, Ferrari, Lamborghini, Maserati, Mercedes, Peugeot, Porsche, Renault, Rolls-Royce, Saab, Volkswagen, Volvo.

This is probably one of the best independent dealers in Europe. They have a large inventory of all makes and models of German, Italian, and British vehicles. They are very honest, courteous, and helpful. Ask for Mr. Mark Tuffin. Write for a free catalog list and prices.

Tax Free Cars
P. C. T.
Ljzerlann   1
2008 Antwerp
Belgium

Telephone: 03-231-5900
Telex: 3-5-546-PH   CART B

Specialties: Alfa Romeo, Audi, BMW, Ferrari, Jaguar, Maserati, Peugeot, Porsche, Renault, Rolls-Royce, Saab, Volkswagen, Volvo.

Tax Free Cars deals mainly with clients from Miami. They are familiar primarily with Florida's laws, regulations, and conversion centers. They are reluctant to deal with buyers from the West Coast because they have no contacts with conversion centers there. I suggest that California residents skip this dealership, but others on the East Coast may want to talk with them.

Mercedes and Porsche Cars
Frans Billen
St. Truidersteenweg   298
Hasselt-Zuid
Belgium
(About 75 miles northeast of Brussels.)

Telephone: 011-27-2344
Telex: 39-875   (Bil Bom)

This is a modern showroom featuring new and used cars and beautiful antique cars. It is worth visiting, though bargains may be difficult to find here.

Dealerships

Linack Automobile
Nymphenburger Strabe   75
8000 Munich   19
West Germany

Telephone: 089-18-5273
Telex: 52-9219

Specialties: Mercedes, Porsche, BMW, and used cars.

This dealership does business with many Americans. They do not have a very large inventory, but the cars they do have are generally very good.

Auto Becker
Suitbertusstrabe   150, Postf.   1440
4000 Dusseldorf   1
West Germany

Telephone: 0211-33-80-1
Telex: 08582-874

Specialties: Mercedes, Porsche, BMW, and Rolls-Royce.

Auto Becker is a good place to buy a new car. Their prices and service are good.

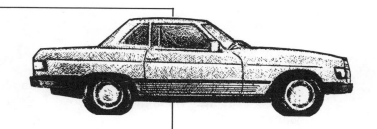

GERMANY

Trasco Export GMBH
Steindamm 38
2820 Bremen 77
West Germany

Telephone: 0049-421-6363-988
Telex: 24-66-24 Trasc D

Affiliated with:

Trasco International Ltd.
Grabenacker Str. 59
6312 Stein Hausen
Switzerland

Telephone: 0041-42-3677-70
Telex: 865318-TRAS CH

Here you also can find special cars like the 500 SEC Gullwing, or the 1000 SEL standard and 30-inch extension limousines. Stock lists are available from Switzerland.

Weiland Auto MBH
Mainzer Landstr. 275
190465 6000 Frankfurt Main
West Germany

Telephone: 49-69-73-1099
Telex: 4-189-081 CARS-D

Specialty: Mercedes.

They have a beautiful showroom. Mr. Harold Weiland has sold thousands of cars to Americans. His service is outstanding.

Dealerships

THE NETHERLANDS

Shipside Tax Free Cars B.V.
P. O. Box 7568
1118 ZH Amsterdam Airport
The Netherlands

Telephone: (020) 152-833
Telex: 12568

Specialties: Alfa Romeo, Audi, BMW, Jaguar, Mercedes, Porsche, Renault, Rolls-Royce, Saab, Volkswagen.

Shipside offers good deals on cars and motorcycles. Write for a free catalog.

Intercorp Europe
56, Boutens Laan
5615 Kt Eindhoven
The Netherlands

Telephone: 40-550055
Telex: 59231

Specialties: Alfa Romeo, Audi, BMW, Mercedes, Peugeot, Porsche, Renault, Saab, Volkswagen, Volvo.

More good bargains to be found here, too. Their service is professional and reputable. Write for free catalog and price lists.

Europe Tax Free Cars
Vliegveldweg 30
Rotterdam Airport (Zestienhoven)
The Netherlands

Telephone: 0101-623077
Telex: 25071 EP CAR NL

Specialties: Alfa Romeo, Audi, BMW, Jaguar, Mercedes, Porsche, Renault, Rolls-Royce, Saab, Volkswagen, Ferrari, Lamborghini, Maserati.

This might be a good place to buy a recreational vehicle, a jeep, or a bus. Write for a free catalog.

MONACO

British Motors
15 Blvd. Princesse-Charlotte
Monte-Carlo
Principality of Monaco   98000

Telephone: 93-50-64-84
Telex: 46-94-75   MC

Specialties: New and used cars; all makes and models of Bentleys and Jaguars.

It might surprise you but, due to the strong value of the U.S. dollar against the French franc, you will find some very good buys here.

You will find good deals on any make or model Rolls-Royce including the Phantom VI limousine. (See chapter 10, *Converting Your Car*, for important information if you are planning to purchase a nonconforming Rolls-Royce.) You may call or write them for stock lists.

Should you want or need further assistance with any aspect of your transaction while in Europe or want references on any of the dealers or individuals with whom you are dealing, I recommend that you contact the following independent European automobile broker:

Mr. Borjan Nakicenovic
Mainzerlandstrasse 275
6000 Frankfurt   1

Telephone: 011 (49)-69686243

Mr. Nakicenovic has specialized in the export of European cars to the United States for a number of years and is familiar with payment procedures, export documents, European vehicle titles and shipping in addition to being very knowledgeable on the different makes and models of European autos and their respective current market prices.

MERCEDES-BENZ 500 SEL •

3

ORDERING YOUR CAR

When ordering your car, you either choose a vehicle from the dealer's inventory or—if you can wait—you order a car to your exact specifications. Many European cars are not easy to find because of the high local demand for them and, in the case of some of the very special cars mentioned in chapter 5, because of limited production. Delivery time for most cars that you order will run to three months or more. If you want a specific car with specific options, order it in advance. You could be very disappointed if you traveled to Europe in the expectation of finding exactly the car you want in some dealer's inventory. You might have to travel to many dealers with no guarantee of finding what you are looking for.

PHONE | MAIL | TELEX

You may order your vehicle by phone, by telex, by mailing the dealer an order form, or by visiting the showroom in person. But I cannot emphasize enough, if you plan to drive the car in Europe, and if you are particular about the options you want, you should not plan to order or find the car in person once you have arrived in Europe. You could spend your entire vacation traveling from dealership to dealership in a rented car.

Ordering Options

The meanings of "standard options" and "fully loaded" are different in Europe and the United States. All European cars manufactured for distribution in the United States are ordered to the specifications of the manufacturer's U.S. representative. They are then distributed to dealers across the country. This means that all the standard equipment on a "fully loaded" made-for-America car will not necessarily be the same as the equipment on a "fully loaded" European car.

For example, the standard equipment ordered by the U.S. manufacturer's representative for a Mercedes 500SEC will include the electric sun roof, climatic air conditioning, power windows (front and rear), AM/FM stereo cassette, etc. The same car when ordered in Europe will not necessarily include such options in the standard price.

"FULLY LOADED"

To avoid any disappointments or problems, you should always order your car referring to the options code lists issued by the manufacturer. Be sure to include all the code options on your car order. Don't order a car with "standard" equipment because you won't know what you are getting. It varies tremendously throughout Europe. If there is a specific car that you want, ask to have the options enumerated by code so you know exactly what you are paying for. This is another area where you shouldn't make any assumptions. For more information on ordering accessories, see chapter 4.

TRANSATLANTIC NEGOTIATIONS

Begin your correspondence with dealers as early as possible. European dealers are very experienced in responding to American inquiries using mail, telephone and telex. Most have catalogues of price lists and will mark those vehicles which are available immediately, as well as those you may have to wait for.

You'll be surprised at the rapport you can develop through letters, telex and phone. European dealers are used to never "meeting" their clients, and will soon put you at ease if they are experienced at what they are doing. They will thoroughly explain all procedures, and send you all forms. Double check with recommendations in this book to be sure you are getting the services you should expect.

What about bargaining and the fine art of negotiations? Well, truthfully, this is always more successful and easier to do well when you are in Europe conversing face to face. But there is no harm in trying and you might meet with some measure of success if you make reasonable offers over the phone. This depends on supply and demand, dealership policy, and most importantly, the personalities involved, so I won't even hazard a guess as to how successful you'll be. But, if your offer is reasonable and polite, you won't alienate the dealer, so do feel free to try.

BEGIN EARLY

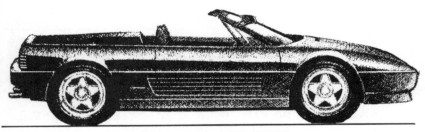

25%/30% DOWN

MAKING A DEPOSIT

As a general rule, when you place an order, a minimum deposit of 25 percent of the car's value is required. The balance must be paid 15 days prior to the final delivery or shipment. For vehicles with special equipment such as air conditioning or a low compression engine, a deposit of 30 percent of the total value may be required.

The deposit is usually made in cash or cashier's check. Of course, you don't send any money before having a signed contract specifying point by point the exact car you are buying, the price, the code list options, dates of delivery, what services they offer, and any special arrangements you have agreed upon. It's advisable that you confirm that the dealer will arrange shipping and marine insurance at this time. Once you have everything spelled out, you can feel confident in making a deposit with a reputable dealer.

I understand that it is not easy to trust a complete stranger, and send money, especially outside the country. You are dealing with international finance; it is part of your new venture, and to some extent, you will have to cope with it. You'll find that methods such as an international letter of credit will help while you develop a positive trans-atlantic business relationship with your dealer.

Here are some suggestions on how to cope with this situation. First of all, the safest way to handle a private importation is to go directly to Europe, find a vehicle of your choice, have your bank wire you the money, and buy the car. But, you'll need to have plenty of time to search for your vehicle, or be lucky enough to quickly find a vehicle of your choice. And let's face it, most of us won't have the time to search out the car of our dreams.

That leaves two possible alternatives:

- **You can order your car in advance and then pick it up in Europe. (This is a good idea, especially if you are very specific in what you are looking for.) I advise you to place a small deposit (either 25 percent or $5,000 is usually required) through the mail on the car of your choice with a reputable dealer in Europe. Then take a cashier's check in U.S. dollars with you to pick up the car once you've arrived in Europe.**

- **You can order your car and have it shipped directly to your home state. In this case, either place a 25 percent deposit and cover the balance with a letter of credit, or, if the dealer agrees, make your entire payment by a letter of credit. Keep in mind that a letter of credit may take up to three or four days to turn around before everything has been cleared. This means that once your dealer receives your letter of credit, your branch bank in Europe (or the bank the dealer wants to deal with in Europe) will need a few days to get the cash against your letter of credit.**

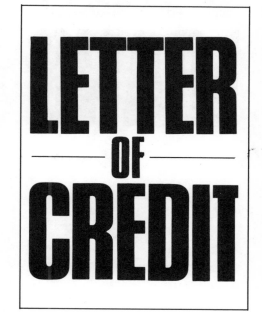

It's a dealer's market, and they don't necessarily want to be tied up waiting for payments on a car that could readily be sold to other customers. So oftentimes they will want direct payments rather than waiting for a letter of credit. At the very least, they'll usually want some form of upfront deposit to show your good faith.

If you wish to place an order for a vehicle with unusual color combinations or unusual options, you may be required to make a higher deposit. This is really very reasonable when you realize that the dealer doesn't know you, and doesn't want to risk being stuck with a personalized vehicle, if you should cancel your order.

Buying a car through private importation does have the drawback of a lack of available financing. You'll have to purchase your car with your own money or through private financing, as banks generally will not give loans for importations.

I strongly advise that you avoid sending cash payments, except as deposit once your contract is in hand, to your dealer in Europe. Once you have turned your cash over to him you will have very little leverage in dealing with him if there should be a delay in delivery of your car or if the car does not exactly meet your specifications.

There are three fairly standard methods of international payments. I think you can feel comfortable using whichever method works best for you.

- **INTERNATIONAL LETTER OF CREDIT:**
  This is the method I recommend for both ease and timing, as well as security. This is a letter from your bank or the bank who will issue you the letter of credit asking that the holder of the letter (your European dealer) be allowed to draw specified sums of money from other banks or agencies to be charged to your (the buyer's) account. You have to apply and complete a form before the letter of credit is issued (it usually takes four days); your funds will then be tied up (but will earn interest) until the supplier (European dealer) performs in accordance with your stipulations. A letter of credit is irrevocable. The only reason your letter of credit would be cancelled is if the dealer does not perform as stipulated in the letter, i.e., doesn't meet vehicle specifications or delivery dates. Remember that this method requires an application and will cost you money. Most banks charge on the average of $200 to establish an international letter of credit. However, while your money is tied up by this credit, you earn interest, so if your whole transaction takes three months from start to finish, you will have that three month's accumulated interest to work with. I would suggest that you inquire at your specific bank concerning their fees and interest schedule.

- **DIRECT PAYMENTS:**
  Available through major banks. You can make your payments with a banker's check or an international bank money order. When timing is important, you can make your payments by telex. If you have complete confidence in your dealer, this is an easy, direct method of doing business, but not one I would recommend if you are new at importation.

- **BANK DRAFT OR ESCROW ACCOUNT:**
  This method allows your bank, or preferably your bank's European branch (in the city of your European dealership), to hold your money in an escrow account. The bank, the dealer and you agree that the money will only be released when the dealer shows proper documentation, proving that he has performed all services negotiated. This is oftentimes the method of choice for those leery of dealing internationally with unknown dealers.

  For example, if you order a car in Frankfurt, you should have the deposit money transferred to your bank's branch office in Frankfurt. The money will be held in an escrow account in your name. The bank will advise your dealer in Frankfurt to place your order and will not release any funds until all the terms and conditions of the escrow have been met. Your dealer then has the assurance that he will be paid if he delivers the right car on time. You will have no problem getting your money back if your dealer does not perform as promised. Also, you get to keep the interest your money earns while you wait for your vehicle.

Be sure to choose the method of payment which will be most favorable to you. How you pay for the car will depend on the fluctuation of the U.S. dollar against the currency of the country in which you are buying it. For example, in Germany payments can be made in West German marks or in any other currency. The currency will be converted to West German marks at the official exchange rate on the day it is received. Payment can be made by bank transfer, certified check, money order, traveler's checks and, of course, cash. Personal checks are only accepted at least six weeks prior to the date of delivery. Your knowledge of foreign currency exchange rates and your skill in juggling currencies can add to the money you save when buying your car abroad. Don't hesitate to ask a knowledgeable friend or friendly banker for help with foreign currencies, as this will greatly impact on your overall savings.

If you order your car by phone, telex, or mail, upon receipt of your letter of confirmation and your deposit, the dealer will send you the following documents:

- A copy of the *purchase order* which is a confirmation of your order and an official receipt for your deposit.

- A *power of attorney* document or similar authorization to be signed by you and notarized. This will enable the dealer to act as your representative in obtaining all necessary documents such as title, registration and tourist plates.

- *Ministry of Finance forms* to be completed by you and then stamped by an embassy or consulate of the country where you have purchased the vehicle. You will have to return these forms to the dealer with a photocopy of the first five pages of your passport. If you are not traveling at the time of this transaction, then the dealer will need your passport number. These forms may be needed to qualify you for tax exemptions and tax-free registration.

Always get a proof of ownership before paying the balance due on the purchase of your car. The dealer should include in your proof of ownership the vehicle identification number (V.I.N.) which is your guarantee that the dealer actually has *your* car in *your* name.

A TYPICAL DEALER'S ORDER FORM • PAGE 47 ➡

Remember to specify options and accessories by code numbers. Be sure you understand all the conditions or rules before you sign and return the form to your dealer.

TRANSCO
SOCIETE ANONYME - NAAMLOZE VENNOOTSCHAP

NOORDERLAAN 95 - 2030 ANTWERP-BELGIUM - PHONES (03) 542 62 40 (10 LINES) - TELEX 35207 TRANS.B

CAR ORDER

N° J 1622

CUSTOMER'S NAME, ADDRESS

CURRENCY

CAR - MAKE

TYPE - DOORS

HP - DIN - CC

1st COLOUR/TRIM

2nd COLOUR/TRIM

DELIVERY DATE - PLACE

BELGIAN TRANSIT PLATES

ROAD INSURANCE

TRANSPORT TO

TRANSPORT INSURANCE

DELIVERY CHARGES

EXTRA OPTIONS

Way of payment :

| TOTAL |
| DEPOSIT |
| BALANCE |

REMARKS

SALES CONDITIONS

Car is to be registered in buyers name and deliverd with travel documents and insurance as specified, valid only in countries specified in policy.

2. Car will be warranted by the factory and the standard manufacturer's warrant will be issued to the purchaser.

3. All payments are to be made in Belgian Francs or its equivalent in foreign currencies acceptable at the official rates at the time of payment.

4. At the time of placing an order, a deposit of minimum 25 % of the total car's value is needed.

5. Final delivery price is liable to readjustment following the transit price at the day of delivery.

6. Balance due is to be paid 15 days before delivery or shipment.

7. All deposits and payments are to be made out to

Generale Bank Maatschappij
(Société Générale de Banque)
Noorderlaan 111 — 2030 Antwerp
Acc. N° 220-0992380-09

Continental Bank
Kipdorp 10 — 2000 Antwerp
Acc. N° 590-5011103-12

8. TRANSCO S.A. is not responsible for delays due to reasons beyond its reasonable control, such as war, strikes, riots, shipping delays, factory production delays and revisions of law or other events beyond its control, and, in such cases, the collection date shall be correspondingly postponed.

CUSTOMER'S SIGNATURE

For TRANSCO N.V. - BELGIUM

Read and approved
DATE _____ PLACE _____   DATE _____ PLACE _____

4

ORDERING ACCESSORIES

WAVE BANDS

Due to the strength of the U.S. dollar against all European currencies at this time, you also can save as much as 40 percent or more by buying these options in Europe.

RADIO

If you buy your car's radio in Europe, be certain that it is equipped with U.S. wave bands. European radios have different wave bands.

ALARM SYSTEM

I strongly recommend that you install your car's alarm system in Europe if you plan to drive the car while there. A high-priced vehicle such as the one you will be buying is always a target for thieves, especially when foreigners are traveling on the continent. For a small expense and significant savings, you can travel and sleep safely. You will also avoid unnecessary delays and grief on your vacation.

If your dealer cannot provide you with a radio or an alarm system, you should find a competent center that installs these extras. You can find these centers all over Europe. In fact, their prices may be lower than those offered by your dealer.

A competent center for the installation of these extras found in Germany and throughout Europe is BOSCH. They are extremely reliable. Here is one of their centers which you can contact to get an address for an outlet near your particular location.

BOSCH
Meinburk Meineke   6MbH
Seidlstr   13–15
8 Munich   2
West Germany

Telephone: 55-163-0

Code List Options

As I mentioned earlier, other accessories and options are best ordered when placing your order for your car using your vehicle's manufacturers code list. Ask your dealer to send you a list of code list options so you can accurately order your accessories.

Taxes

There is no additional tax on factory optional equipment which was included in your total purchase price (i.e., which you ordered in advance).

When you purchase additional equipment such as a radio or alarm system during your trip, ask the seller to give you (as a foreigner) the value added tax (V.A.T.) refund papers. When you leave the country where the tax was paid (either by car or at the airport) show them the V.A.T. papers. You will either get an on-the-spot refund or it will be sent to your home. Remember, though, this has nothing to do with shipping your car. This applies only to purchases for your car made while traveling throughout Europe.

V.A.T. PAPERS

LAMBORGHINI COUNTACH S

THE SPECIAL CARS

This chapter has been included for those who simply must have more than the top of the line. It is for those who want to be noticed on Rodeo Drive in Beverly Hills or Worth Avenue in Palm Beach. It is for car lovers who want a one-of-a-kind automobile. The addresses included here should satisfy even the most discriminating clientele.

Since every one of these cars is modified individually in accordance with the desires of each car owner, you will have to contact the modifiers for more information about the time and the prices involved in modifying your car.

I have listed here some very reliable modifiers of special cars and their specialties, although they are capable of developing many different cars. To import these cars through dealerships in the United States is outrageously expensive, if not impossible, so for many, private importation is the only method available.

Just to clarify, in this case we are talking about modifying cars to your personal needs and standards. We are not talking about conversion and modification of these cars to meet United States DOT and EPA standards which is another step you must take.

If you are seriously interested in purchasing a special car, write to these addresses and tell them of your specific interests and needs in having them create a special car for you.

In all likelihood, they will send you beautiful full-color catalogs complete with photographs, explanations and price lists.

Once you have come closer to choosing exactly what you want, visit your U.S. conversion center (see chapter 10 for those I recommend). You may have to contact many conversion centers to find one that is equipped and interested in converting your special car to meet EPA and DOT standards. I cannot stress enough how important it is in the case of special cars, that you check with your U.S. conversion center *first*. It is much more difficult and expensive to convert these cars to U.S. standards.

Once you have an agreement with a reputable U.S. conversion center, then buy a standard car in Europe and arrange to have it delivered to the European special car modifier. This is much less expensive than buying the standard car to be modified from the special car dealer.

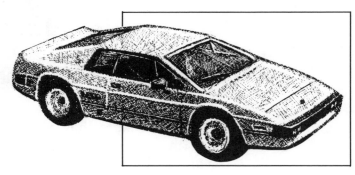

European Modifiers for Special Cars

The modifiers below are listed in alphabetical order.

Alpina
Alpina Burkard Bovensiepen K.G.
Alpenstrasse 37
8938 Buchloe
West Germany
(Buchloe is about 40 miles west of Munich.)

Telephone: 08241-3071

Specialty: all BMW models.

They will modify the engine and the suspension; add aerodynamic accessories, wheels, seats, and exterior decoration.

AMG
AMG Motorenbau GMBH
Daimlerstrasse 1
7151 Affalterbach
West Germany
(Affalterbach is 15 miles northeast of Stuttgart.)

Telephone: 07144-3119

Since 1967 AMG has been modifying Mercedes-Benz. The quality of their work and their reputation is known throughout the continent.

AMG will modify the 190E, the 230E, the 280E, the 240D Turbo, the 300D Turbo, the 280SE, the 500SE, the 500SEC, and maybe other models. They will transform the engine, the interior, the exterior, the wheels, and the sound system. Their cars are very popular in the United States.

Baur
Karrosserie Baur GMBH
6 Poststrasse 40–62
Berg
West Germany
(Berg is about 15 miles southeast of Munich.)

Telephone: 0711-26-851-51

Baur specializes in modifying BMW models 316, 318i, 320i, 323i into beautiful convertibles.

BB

BB Auto K.G.
Orber Strasse 6
6000 Frankfurt/Main 61
West Germany

Telephone: 0611-41-00-01

BB does precise and exquisite work. Their specialties include: (1) a Porsche 928 convertible; (2) a Mercedes 500SEC electric hardtop convertible; (3) a conversion of a Mercedes 500SEL which integrates the Mercedes 500SEC front; (4) a famous electronic steering wheel. They also modify the Porsche 911SC Targa, the Volkswagen Golf GTI, and the Volkswagen Polo. They modify the engine, the interior, and the exterior of the car.

DP

DP Motorsport
Zum Alten Wasser Werk
5063 Overath 6
West Germany
(Overath is about 15 miles west of Cologne.)

Telephone: 02204-71067

DP Motorsport will modify a basic Porsche Turbo to look like a Porsche 935. They modify the engine, the transmission, the windows, the dimensions, and the exterior of the car. They do beautiful work.

Duchatelet

Duchatelet S.A.
114 Quai du Roi Albert
4020 Liege
Belgium
(Liege is about 100 miles southwest of Brussels.)

Telephone: 41-42-53-34

Duchatelet rebuilds Mercedes including the 500SEL, the 500SEC, and the 190E with ultraluxurious interiors using the most precious woods. They can install televisions, bars, telephones, front and rear consoles, and leather seats of their own design.

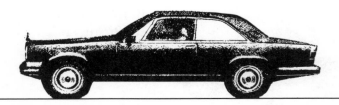

Koenig

R. Koenig   GMBH
Mitterestrasse   3
D-8000 Munich   2
West Germany

Telephone: 089-53-0441
Telex: 528145   Koevm

Mr. Willy Koenig will modify your Ferrari into a very beautiful and special car. He uses parts from Modena, Italy, which are used by competition racers. For the Ferrari aficionado, this is the place.

L'Etoile

Ronny Coach Building Company
Brugsesteenweg   211
B-8242 Oudenburg   (Roksem)
Belgium
(Oudenburg is about 20 miles southeast of Brugges. The closest airport is in Antwerp, 100 miles east.)

Telephone: (050) 81-14-83

L'Etoile will transform a Mercedes 500SEL into a six-door limousine with a long wheel base.

Styling Garage

Styling Garage Handelsges   MBH
Muhlenstrasse   2
D-2080 Pinneberg
West Germany
(Pinneberg is 5 miles north of Hamburg.)

Telephone: 4101-2701718

Styling Garage specializes in transforming Mercedes-Benz. From a 500SEL they create a 600SGS Limousine or a 1000SGS Limousine. A 380SEC or a 500SEC can be converted into a convertible. From a 500SEC they create the famous "Gullwing." And from a 190 they can create a SGS City Fun.

Don't forget that it may be difficult or impossible to make these special cars conform to DOT and EPA standards. The modifications may also cancel your warranty and will make the cars difficult and very expensive to insure. You should investigate all of these points through your U.S. modifier or conversion center *before* buying one of these cars.

PART

II

DRIVING IN EUROPE & SHIPPING YOUR CAR

• MERCEDES-BENZ 500 SEL AMG •

CHAPTER

6

REGISTERING AND DRIVING YOUR CAR IN EUROPE

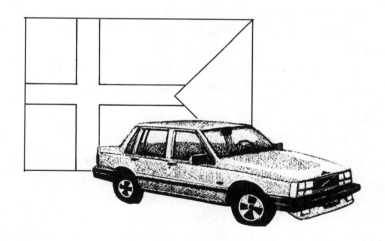

Your dealer should take care of all the paperwork needed to register your car. This includes the titling documents (registration papers), bill of sale proving ownership, and insurance papers. If for some reason your dealer is unwilling to do this, then you will want to avoid the dealership altogether. Go to a more competent and cooperative dealer. Usually a day or less is needed for this work. You will then receive transit plates, customs clearance (to prove the car is for export, so it will not be taxed), and all the travel documents you might need. Typically the cost of registering the vehicle is included in the price. If not, it is sure to be no more than a nominal amount which varies from country to country. An average is about $85 U.S. in Germany.

In order to obtain the title and registration of the vehicle in your name, you must authorize your dealer to take all the necessary steps before you arrive to pick up the car. For this you will, of course, have had to send him your power of attorney. The transit plates will entitle you to drive your car in Europe without paying duties or the value added tax (V.A.T.).

The period of validity of most countries' Ministry of Finance International Tax-free Registration varies from two months to one year, depending on your particular circumstances. Once you have received your registration, transit plates, and travel documents, it is very important that you carefully check the date of issue and expiration. Be sure they cover the full length of your trip or longer if you want flexibility. Do not drive your car in Europe after the plates or insurance have expired.

Every time you cross a border, the customs officers will check your registration papers and insurance. (See chapter 7, *Insuring Your Car in Europe*.) They must be valid. If they have expired, customs will confiscate your car and hold it until you can produce valid papers.

Your own valid U.S. driver's license is recognized practically all over Western Europe. You should get an international driver's license if you plan to drive in any of the Eastern European countries. You can obtain an international driver's license through your local automobile club or association. All you will need is your valid driver's license and two passport-size photographs.

Driving In Europe

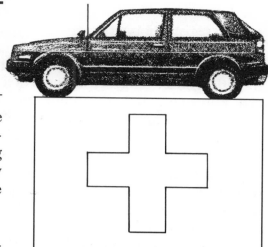

While it is not the purpose of this book to give a course on driving in Europe, there are some basics that I'd be remiss in not sharing with you. With all my European driving experience, I do know the rules of the road, and while every country has its own laws and driving habits, there are some general guidelines which you would do well to observe.

SAFETY

You really need to be aware at all times that you are not driving in the United States. Sometimes just getting behind the wheel lulls you into a familiar state of mind, so be especially alert to international road signs, speed limits and driving courteously. Remember, too, that your international driving encompasses a language barrier so be sure you familiarize yourself with roadside terminology in each country.

Drive safely. Drive soberly. In Europe, you are automatically put in jail if you drive drunk. Needless to say, don't carry any illegal drugs on you or in your car in Europe. If you are stopped by police, be courteous and cooperative. The last thing you want to do is antagonize a foreign police officer, and sometimes unfortunately, just being a tourist puts you in a less than popular position.

When passing through customs, be very serious. Customs officials don't fool around at all. Answer their questions politely and honestly, have your papers in order, and everything will go smoothly.

SPEED LIMITS

In Germany, there is no speed limit on most of the *autobahns* (highways). Be very careful of the fast drivers, as they are really flying. The California freeways will seem tame when compared with Germany and France. If you are a slow driver (under 80 miles per hour!), don't drive in the fast lane (far left lane). You will literally be run off the road.

In France, particularly in Paris, the faint of heart should seriously consider taking a taxi. Paris roads are a real zoo. For that matter, the major cities in Italy are just as difficult to drive in. I'd hate to think of your having a fender bender or worse in your beautiful new car, so I do think you should give serious consideration to not driving in these cities. It's difficult even for the residents, but as a tourist dealing with strange roads, strange languages, uncertain destinations, strange regulations plus the very wild driving habits which prevail in these cities, I'd recommend taxis and other forms of public transportation.

DRIVING IN COMMUNIST COUNTRIES

Be prepared to spend a few extra hours or more at the border crossings when entering a communist country. And again, be polite, honest, and have all necessary papers in order.

Be sure your insurance coverage includes travel in communist countries.

Inquire at their consulate or embassy before entering a communist country in your own car. They will outline their requirements and regulations, as well as any other information you should be aware of.

For example, in Yugoslavia you need to purchase tickets in order to purchase gasoline at gas stations. They sell the tickets on main streets and along highways. Some communist countries, like the U.S.S.R., have extremely strict regulations limiting tourists in private cars, so check this out carefully when you are planning your itinerary. You don't want to be turned away at a border crossing.

But I don't mean to discourage you from driving in communist countries. It gives you exposure and experience of another lifestyle that you just can't grasp on group tours. And places like Prague, Czechoslovakia, and the Dalmation coast of Yugoslavia are breathtakingly beautiful.

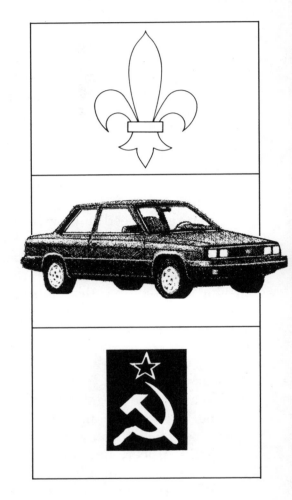

When driving in Europe, there are some general things to remember which will help you have a safe trip in your new car.

- **SAFETY EQUIPMENT**
  When traveling in Europe, you should always equip your vehicle with:

  > First aid kit
  > Set of tools
  > Set of fuses
  > Flares
  > Flashlight and batteries
  > Towing rope
  > Jumper cables
  > Fire extinguisher (cannot be shipped by air)
  > Extra set of keys

  When you ship your car to the United States, do not leave the safety equipment in the car. Always ship loose articles separately (see chapter 8, *Shipping Your Car to the United States*).

- Always carry a **TRANSLATION BOOK**

- **MAPS**

- **ADDRESSES OF YOUR INSURANCE REPRESENTATIVE'S BRANCH OFFICES** throughout Europe in case of accidents.

- **ADDRESSES OF AUTHORIZED CAR REPAIR SHOPS for your make and model vehicle. Your dealer will provide you with a list if you remember to ask.**

- **If you need any help, contact the U.S. Embassy, if possible. Any tourism office can help with less major concerns.**

- **Don't overlook the concierge at any of the major hotels. They always speak English and are well-versed in dealing with the types of questions and problems you are apt to have. They are particularly helpful if you find you are in need at odd hours of the night or during holidays.**

Most importantly, I think you will find that people the world over will be very helpful and friendly to you, if you are courteous and respectful to them. Keep in mind that you are a guest in their country. Your enthusiasm and interest in them will be contagious. That is what makes traveling in Europe—especially by car—such a wonderful experience.

• MERCEDES-BENZ 500 SL AMG •

7

INSURING YOUR CAR FOR EUROPEAN TRAVEL

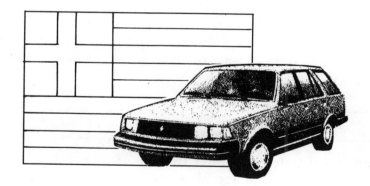

In Europe an automobile cannot be registered unless it has been properly insured for European use. Your dealer can assist you in purchasing insurance. He will provide you with the green insurance card for any kind of insurance your prefer (legal liability, theft, fire, or even for all risks). Generally your dealer will already have a business relationship with American International Underwriters. Their network of claims agents all over Europe can assist you if necessary.

I would not recommend buying your insurance from countries other than Germany, Belgium, and the Netherlands. These countries are rather strict about their insurance, which works to your benefit if something should happen to your car. Germany is especially strict and will not always accept insurance policies from other, more lenient countries. If you insure your car in another country, you may find that you are required to purchase a special insurance policy before you may drive your car in Germany. So, as you can see, if possible, it makes sense to purchase your overseas policy in Germany which will keep you well-covered throughout Europe. If you plan to travel in communist countries, then be sure your insurance is valid there.

General Rules of Insurance

There is a very true saying that no one can ever be insured enough. The best thing for you to do is to make sure that your car is covered for its total value in any circumstances whether it be accident, fire or theft. Get as much insurance coverage as possible. I recommend that you get coverage B–E as shown in Table 7–1. This is not an area where you should try to save a few dollars.

Below are the general rules of insurance established in Germany, the Netherlands, and Belgium. They apply to private passenger cars, station wagons, buses (up to nine passengers), and motorcycles.

AGE LIMITS

- Applicants and/or drivers under the age of twenty-one and over the age of seventy are not eligible.

- Applicants and/or drivers of twenty-one or twenty-two years of age pay a surcharge of 75 percent.

- Applicants and/or drivers of twenty-three and twenty-four years of age pay a surcharge of 50 percent.

- The surcharges will depend on the applicant's age on the day the insurance becomes effective.

TERRITORIAL LIMITS

- Insurance protection is offered and valid throughout Europe (except Turkey) as well as Morocco, Tunisia, and Israel. Motorcycle insurance is not valid for Albania, the U.S.S.R. and its Eastern European satellite countries.

MEDICAL INSURANCE

- Usually an international insurance policy has an upper limit of $1,500 per event and per person in the car at the time of an accident. These $1,500 payments are at first risk; that is to say, the bills for medical treatment will be paid up to this amount even when the operator is at fault for the accident.

SPANISH BAIL BOND

- Upon your request your dealer will provide you with an Amendatory Endorsement to the insurance policy for bail bond and criminal defense coverage valid in Spain. This is very important if you will be driving in Spain.

RECREATIONAL VEHICLE INSURANCE

- Upon request your dealer will supply you with recreational vehicle (caravan) insurance for legal liability including fire and theft. Collision or upset cannot be insured.

SPORTS CAR INSURANCE

- Different rates are applicable to sports cars and only drivers from 25 to 65 years of age are eligible under these rules.

IMPORTANT REMINDERS

- Due to strict customs' rules in Germany, Belgium, Austria, the Netherlands, and communist countries, it is mandatory that you have at least one month's European legal liability insurance if you are driving your car in Europe. This must be purchased through your dealer at the time you buy the car.

- The maximum age of cars insurable under this program is ten years for legal liability insurance and five years for full coverage. This means it may be difficult to find an insurer for a used car. In this case, I suggest you contact American International Underwriters GMBH.

- These rules and regulations may change without notice. Remember, too, that they vary slightly from country to country, and they are strictly enforced.

Do not forget: having no insurance in Europe means your car cannot be registered. Your vehicle will be seized until you can prove that it is properly insured.

For more details regarding the insurance you will purchase, contact your European dealer or write to this address:

American International Underwriters GMBH
Oberlindau   76–78
West Germany
Europe

Telephone: 0611-71-521

HOME DRIVE COVERAGE
(U.S. AND CANADA ONLY)

Home drive coverage protects your car during shipping and after it has arrived in your home state. It is valid for a maximum of 30 days after the car has been picked up at its port of destination. This coverage can only be purchased together with a tourist policy. Simply add one month's premium to the cost of the needed European coverage. If European coverage is purchased for 12 months or more, home drive coverage may be added free of charge if you request it.

I do not recommend that you use this insurance. You can imagine the problems of dealing with an insurance company on another continent if you should be involved in an accident or if your car should be stolen. Instead, purchase European insurance for your travel time, and purchase a marine insurance policy through your shipper or dealer (check the terms yourself) to protect your car during shipping. Make arrangements with your domestic insurance company so your car will be insured from the moment it arrives at its port of destination.

Table 7-1

→

• Pages 72–73

Table 7-1

INSURANCE RATES

CARS, STATION WAGONS & BUSES

RATES ARE QUOTED IN U.S. DOLLARS

GROUP	HORSEPOWER	DEDUCTIBLE	MONTHS					
			1	2	3	4	5	6
A	40	40	55	100	127	160	178	204
B-E	40	40	81	151	191	229	268	306
A	41-50	40	59	112	140	168	196	224
B-E	41-50	40	88	168	211	252	294	337
A	51-60	40	65	122	153	183	215	244
B-E	51-60	40	99	183	229	276	321	367
A	61-70	40	78	142	178	213	255	285
B-E	61-70	40	117	213	268	321	378	428
A	71-80	40	88	163	204	244	283	326
B-E	71-80	40	134	244	306	367	425	488
A	81-90	40	100	183	229	274	321	386
B-E	81-90	40	150	276	343	412	481	578
A	91-100	40	112	204	255	222	356	406
B-E	91-100	40	166	306	382	459	534	612
A	101-120	80	112	204	255	306	356	406
B-E	101-120	80	166	306	382	459	534	612
A	121-150	160	156	285	356	306	499	570
B-E	121-150	160	180	329	411	328	576	855
A	151-200	160	187	347	433	519	606	692
B-E	151-200	160	281	425	650	779	909	1038
A	201-250	160	222	407	510	611	712	815
B-E	201-250	160	333	400	763	917	1070	1222
MEDICAL PAYMENTS			3	3	5	6	7	9
TOWING CHARGES			2.5	2.5	2.5	3	3	3
POLICY FEE			5	5	5	5	5	5

*NOTES TO THE INSURANCE RATES
The prices in this table are for cars, station wagons, and buses up to nine passengers. Insurance rates in Germany, Belgium, and the Netherlands are usually calculated by the horsepower of the vehicle. Engine horsepowers are given in Chapter 2.

Group A: Provides third party liability (compulsory); unlimited coverage except for material damage caused by explosions or fire in which case, coverage is limited to $75,000.

Please Note: This table is provided to give you an approximate idea in U.S. dollars of what insurance will cost in Europe. Dollar prices will change with fluctuations in the exchange rate.

(Continued on next page)

Table 7-1 (continued)

INSURANCE RATES
CARS, STATION WAGONS & BUSES
RATES ARE QUOTED IN U.S. DOLLARS

GROUP	HORSEPOWER	DEDUCTIBLE	MONTHS					
			7	8	9	10	11	12
A	40	40	231	258	287	314	341	371
B–E	40	40	347	388	430	471	513	555
A	41–50	40	254	284	315	345	377	405
B–E	41–50	40	382	427	473	518	565	608
A	51–60	40	278	310	344	377	410	444
B–E	51–60	40	417	466	517	566	616	666
A	61–70	40	323	361	401	440	479	504
B–E	61–70	40	486	544	603	661	720	756
A	71–80	40	370	414	458	503	547	592
B–E	71–80	40	555	622	689	754	820	889
A	81–90	40	396	466	517	566	616	666
B–E	81–90	40	625	605	774	848	925	999
A	91–100	40	462	518	573	629	651	741
B–E	91–100	40	694	777	860	945	976	1111
A	101–120	80	462	518	573	629	651	741
B–E	101–120	80	694	777	860	945	976	1111
A	121–150	160	648	726	803	881	980	1037
B–E	121–150	160	972	1089	1206	1322	1470	1556
A	151–200	160	786	881	975	1072	1163	1145
B–E	151–200	160	1180	1322	1463	1600	1744	1717
A	201–250	160	925	1037	1146	1259	1370	1482
B–E	201–250	160	1388	1556	1719	1888	2055	15223
MEDICAL PAYMENTS			10	11	12	14	15	16
TOWING CHARGES			4	4	4	5	5	5
POLICY FEE			5	5	5	5	5	5

*NOTES TO THE INSURANCE RATES

Group B–E: Includes third party liability (as in Group A) plus fire, theft, glass breakage, damage caused by acts of God, material damage to the vehicle regardless of who is at fault, subject to a deductible per accident claim, as listed in table.

Medical Payments: $1,500 per person per accident.

Towing Charge: Up to $35 for each accident.

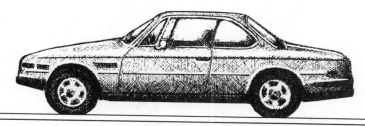

FERRARI 400i 12-CYLINDER SEDAN •

SHIPPING YOUR CAR TO THE UNITED STATES

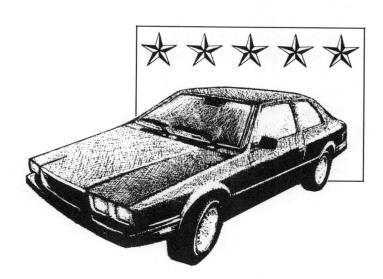

EUR. → U.S.A.

You can ship your car from Europe to the United States by air or by sea. From Europe to the East or West Coasts by air takes from four days to two weeks, depending on how busy the airlines are and the schedules of the airline you use. Shipment by sea takes from two to four weeks. In general the procedure and conditions by air and by sea are the same. However, since shipping your car by air is so expensive, this chapter will emphasize shipment by sea. This is the method virtually everyone will use.

BY SEA

Shipping an automobile by sea is certainly the most popular and the least expensive way to go. Table 8–1 will give you some idea of the cost of shipping different vehicles to different destinations. The prices in the table are an average of the prices charged by the major shipping companies and are in U.S. dollars. If you choose to arrange your own shipping (rather than have a dealer make the arrangements), I have listed reliable shipping companies in this chapter.

> If the maximum liability is based on the weight of the car, *make sure there will be enough coverage to protect you from total loss of the vehicle.*

BY AIR

Shipping a car by air is, of course, much more expensive but much faster than shipping by sea. You can save two to three weeks if you're in a great hurry to have your new car. The major airlines for such shipments presently are KLM and Lufthansa.

To give you an idea of the costs involved, to ship a Mercedes 500SEL from Amsterdam by KLM would cost $2,2022 U.S. to New York and $2,789 U.S. to Los Angeles. The insurance rate is ten cents (U.S.) per $100 (U.S.) of value. Maximum liability is $20 per kilogram.

To ship the same car from Frankfurt on Lufthansa would cost $2,272 U.S. to Boston or New York and $2,727 U.S. to Los Angeles. The insurance rate is $1.50 (U.S.) per $1,000 (U.S.) value. Maximum liability up to the total value insured (which means there is no limit to the value they will insure).

If you decide to ship your car by air, contact the cargo department of the airline of your choice. If the maximum liability is based on the weight of the car, *make sure there will be enough coverage to protect you from total loss of the vehicle.*

Table 8-1
→
• Pages 78–79

Table 8-1

SEA FREIGHTS

EUROPE TO NORTH AMERICA

RATES ARE QUOTED IN U.S. DOLLARS

MAKE & MODEL	DESTINATION	
	HALIFAX NOVA SCOTIA MONTREAL	NEW YORK NEWARK
ALFA ROMEO	500–667	450–614
AUDI 80	605	555
100, 200	658	608
BMW 316, 318, 320, 323	610	560
518, 520, 525, 528, 628, 633, 635	657	607
728, 732, 735, 745	722	672
FERRARI 308GTSi, GTB	570	520
JAGUAR XJSHE	710	660
MERCEDES 230SL, 280SL, 350SL, 380SL, 450SL, 500SL	700	650
180, 190, 200, 230, 250, 280, 280E, 190D, 200D, 220D, 240D, 300D, 240TD, 280TD, 300TD, 230C, 280C, 300CTD, 280CE, 280SLC, 350SLC, 450SLC, 450SLC5.0, 500SLC	750	700
220S, 230S, 250S, 280S, 220SE, 230SE, 250SE, 280SE, 300SE, 350SE, 380SE, 450SE, 500SE, 250SEC, 280SEC, 300SEC, 380SEC, 500SEC, 220SEL, 300SEL	816	766
300SD, 280SEL, 350SEL, 380SEL, 450SEL, 450SEL6.9, 500SEL	850	800
600	950	900
600 Pullman	1500	1000
PORSCHE 924, Turbo, 944	500	450
911, 928, 930, 912, 914	550	500
VOLKSWAGEN Polo	490	440
Derby, Golf, Scirocco, Rabbit	530	480
Beetle, Jetta, Kharman Ghia	570	520
Passat, Dasher	600	550

Table 8-1. *Generally, shipping companies charge by car size—large, medium, or small. To use this chart, simply find a comparably sized car to approximate your shipping fee.*

Table 8-1 (continued)

SEA FREIGHTS

EUROPE TO NORTH AMERICA

RATES ARE QUOTED IN U.S. DOLLARS

DESTINATION:		
OTHER EAST COAST CITIES (BALTIMORE, PORTSMOUTH)	SOUTH ATLANTIC GULF COAST (JACKSONVILLE, HOUSTON)	WEST COAST (LOS ANGELES, PORTLAND, SAN FRANCISCO, VANCOUVER)
440–604	454–619	560–720
545	559	655
598	612	708
550	564	660
597	611	707
662	676	772
510	524	620
650	664	760
660	654	750
710	704	800
776	770	866
810	804	900
910	904	1000
1010	1004	1100
460	454	550
510	504	600
450	444	540
490	484	580
530	524	620
560	554	650

There are three different methods from which you can choose when shipping your vehicle:

1. The dealer who sold you the car will, at your request, take care of shipping it. If your dealer is unable to do this, he will direct you to someone who can. This is the most efficient method and oftentimes saves you a lot of time and worry. Whether you are in Europe or not, I recommend this method over the others. Even if you have driven through Europe, your dealer will often arrange shipping at a port near your trip's final destination, but you must agree on a *definite* shipping date.

2. Make all the arrangements yourself. If you have the time, this is surely the cheapest way. Basically, shipping the car by yourself means that you take the car directly to the shipping company or to the port. You can drive the car to Antwerp, Rotterdam, Bremerhafen, Hamburg, Emden, or any other port which is convenient for you. Take all the necessary papers with you, as explained in this chapter, and the shipping agent will fill out the forms for you. Doing this for yourself will save you money, particularly if you read this chapter with care.

3. You might consider letting a freight forwarding agent (in Germany: Internationale Spediteur) arrange for the shipment of your car. They will pick up your car in any major city in Europe. They will take care of all shipping arrangements including taking it to the actual shipping company at the port. Of course, you will pay for this service. It will cost you at least $300 U.S., depending on the type of vehicle you have and the exchange rates at the time. Needless to say, due to the additional expense, this method is recommended only as a last resort. And you should also be aware that at least 80 percent of the time, when you use a freight forwarding agent, you will end up shipping under consolidation which I do not recommend. Check carefully that this will not be the case if you use a freight forwarding agent.

> *I strongly recommend that only your vehicle and only your name (as the importer) appear on the bill of lading.*

DON'T SHIP UNDER CONSOLIDATION!

I must strongly urge you to avoid shipping your car under consolidation! Consolidation basically means that your vehicle is shipped and processed as part of a group, rather than individually (with *only* your name on the bill of lading). For example, most freight forwarding agencies in Europe will list as many as one hundred cars on the bill of lading. This means that the notification of arrival for all 100 cars is on the same bill of lading. In addition, all 100 cars must go through one major customs house broker at the port of destination, a very time-consuming process. Your personal customs house broker will have to go through this group broker in order to release your car. It will involve at least three or four more days and no small amount of confusion.

I strongly recommend that only your vehicle and only your name (as the importer) appear on the bill of lading (B/L). In addition, on the bill of lading under "person to be notified or agent at port of destination" be sure your *personal* customs house broker's name, address and telephone number are listed. This is without a doubt the best and fastest way to release your vehicle from customs to the conversion center, taking you one giant step closer to taking full stateside possession of your car.

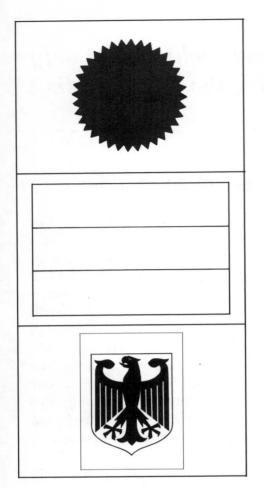

Reliable Shipping Companies

If you decide to ship your car personally rather than letting your dealer handle all the details, you should contact the shipping companies listed below. They are all reliable and helpful.

Econopak Transcar
Speditionsgesellschaft   MBH
Landsberger Strabe   191A
8000 Munich   21
West Germany

Telephone: (089) 57-20-77
Telex: 5215232

Affiliated with offices in:

Frankfurt — Telephone: (0611) 690 2518
Telex: 4170201
Geneva — Telephone: (022) 96 5511
Telex: 22061
Zurich — Telephone: 1-7401111
Telex: 56293
London — Telephone: 1-5156684
Telex: 893546
Brussels — Telephone: (02) 513 4150
Telex: 25412
Beirut — Telephone: 480260-481272
Telex: 40109   LE

Transship GMBH
Burgermeister-Smidt-Strabe   58/60
2800 Bremen   1
West Germany

Telephone: (0421) 14264
Telex: 246584   Trans D

Affiliated with an office in:

Hamburg — Telephone: (040) 373703
Telex: 214944   Trans D

Transcar
20 Rue le Sueur
75116 Paris
France

Telephone: 500-03-04
Telex: 610597

Affiliated with offices in:

    Frankfurt
    Geneva
    London
    Munich
    Barcelona
    Nice
    Cannes

Matina France
Entrepots MacDonald
171, Boulevard MacDonald
75019 Paris
France

Telephone: (1) 238-8088
            (1) 238-8189
Telex: 210420 MCD

AMESCO P.V.B.A.
Kribbestraat 9
B-2000 Antwerp
Belgium

Telephone: (03) 231-42-39
           (03) 231-42-38
Telex: 71469 AMESCOB

Rhenus Transport International
Tiefer 2 P.O.B. 102247
2800 Bremen
West Germany

Telephone: 0421-3657-0
Telex: 244-833

If you request it, most of these companies will arrange to pick up your vehicle from any major city in Europe for a very reasonable cost. When you call or write to these shippers for information, be sure to ask if they have an affiliated office in or near your home state. Most of these shipping companies also ship worldwide, if you wish to send your car to some place other than North America.

A Shipping Checklist

Before you turn your car over to anyone for shipment to the United States, you should know the answers to the following questions (ask your dealer to verify these points if he is arranging shipping for you):

- **What will the insurance cost? How reliable is the insurer?**
- **How much advance notice does the shipping company require? Do they guarantee departure dates?**
- **Approximately how long will it take to reach the port of destination once the ship has sailed?**
- **Is the company which is handling the shipping a freight forwarding agent or a shipping company?**
- **What type of vessel is being used? "Roll on, roll off" means that your car is driven from the dock into the ship and driven from the ship to the dock at landing. On a container ship, your car will be inside a container which is lifted onto and off the ship. This is a more expensive method of shipment, but your car is better protected from both the elements and from theft.**

Before the ship containing your car sets sail, you should have received the following documents from your shipping company:

- **Bill of lading**
- **Marine insurance certificate**
- **Steam cleaning certificate**
- **Registration certificate**
- **Certificate of origin**
- **Export formalities such as customs clearance at the port of loading, which the shipping company will take care of for you.**

It is very important, particularly for the bill of lading, that every one of these documents be in your name. Only the person who is named on the bill of lading will be able to take possession of the car once it has arrived at its destination.

If for some reason, you do not receive all the necessary papers, don't panic. Worse could happen! Simply contact your shipping company in Europe or preferably its agent at the port of destination in the United States. Of course, if you work with a customs house broker, which as you can tell I recommend, then the broker will know who to contact and you needn't get involved or be concerned.

It goes without saying that you should read your shipping and marine insurance contracts very carefully — before you sign them! If some essential item has been left out, have it written in. The verbal assurances or addenda which you receive are worth nothing, so get everything in writing.

LEGALITIES AND NECESSARY PRECAUTIONS

The following papers and materials are needed to process an automobile out of Europe:

- **Registration card**
  It is very important that you give only a *copy* of your Registration Card. *Always keep the original yourself*. **It is as important as your passport. You will need the original registration card in order to register your car in the United States. No copies will be accepted.**

  If you lose your original registration card or give it away, the Department of Motor Vehicles (in the U.S.) will require a Motor Vehicle Bond which will cost several hundred dollars. You would need to secure this from your insurance company.

- **Green insurance card**

- **Customs documents, if any**
  This will be a document proving that the vehicle is for export. Also, when your payment for duty is refunded, you will receive a document stating that the vehicle is for export.

- **A complete *set of keys***

These documents are the things they will generally ask for at the shipping company. Take all your papers and documents to avoid any delays, if you are arranging your own shipping.

Marine or Air Insurance

You absolutely must purchase or have your dealer arrange to purchase a marine or air insurance policy prior to shipping your car. Some shippers are not liable for loss or damage to your car or its contents. Others claim to have insurance, but it is generally for a limited amount. You must have full coverage including denting, theft, fire, and total loss up to the full value of your vehicle.

Be certain that your marine or air insurance takes effect from the moment you leave your car at the airport or the docks. Also be certain that your insurance covers your car while it is being stored on the docks and while it is being transported into and out of the ship.

Do not purchase "port to port" insurance. "Port to port" protects you only while your car is inside the ship. It does not protect you while your car is on the dock or being moved into or out of the ship. To repeat, your car must be insured from the time you leave it with the shipper (or anyone who will take it to the port) until the time you pick it up in the United States.

Before your car leaves Europe and in your presence (or your dealer's representative's), your vehicle will be inspected. Any irregularities, dents, or damage of any kind, including missing parts, will be noted on a report. Read the report carefully. A copy of this report will be sent to your marine insurance company.

Marine insurance should always be placed with one of the leading international underwriters. Since most European automobile dealers can get a cheaper insurance rate than you can get on your own, you should let your dealer arrange for your insurance. Before you buy your car from a dealer, make sure he can perform this service for you. Many dealers cannot or will not do this for you. Also, any major shipper should be able to sell you marine insurance. If not, you should question its reliability and professionalism, and probably find another shipper. Be sure you verify that the insurance they provide is as thorough as I recommend.

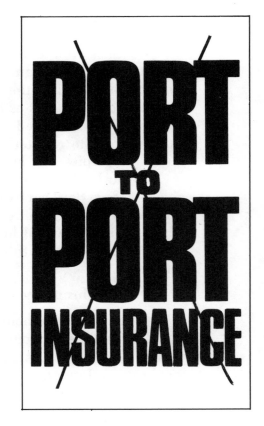

INSURANCE CO$T

The cost of your marine insurance will depend on the shipping company and the insurance company you use. It will vary between 1 and 1.5 percent of the total value of the car plus the sea freight. It will also vary for each port of destination. For Canada and the Great Lakes it could run as high as 2.3 percent of the value of the car and the sea freight.

The marine insurance rate for radios, trailers, and motorcycles is double that for cars. The value of these items will have to be listed separately. Keep in mind that if the car is insured with a deductible, the deductible also will apply to the radio.

In some cases, marine insurance without a deductible is only available for new cars that are less than two years old. Older cars are usually insured with a deductible of $150 to $500.

The shipping company and your insurance company will not accept any liability for the mechanical condition of the car or for defects to the engine. Please be aware of possible damage to the engine due to changes in temperature. The cooling system must be protected with a nonalcoholic permanent type antifreeze solution testing to minus twenty degrees Fahrenheit or lower if necessary. All vehicles being shipped between September and April must comply with this condition.

If any special parts have been added to your car, they should be listed separately and insured.

Maritime insurance should be written for the total value of your car plus freight charges. Make sure that the insurance company is very reliable and is endorsed by the shipping company. If you are using a shipping agent, you should not accept his word alone that the insurance company is reliable. Check with the shipping company itself.

Your marine insurance should cease at the end of ten days from the date of the vehicle's landing at its port of destination.

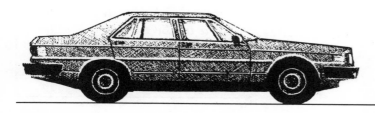

STEAM CLEANER

To safeguard against the importation of dangerous pests, the U.S. Department of Agriculture requires that the undercarriage of imported cars be free from foreign soil. Have your car thoroughly steam cleaned by the shipper before shipment. This should be included in your shipping fee as part of your contract. Get a certificate from the shipper to certify that this work has been done.

PERSONAL BELONGINGS

Your automobile is not a shipping container. For your own safety, do not use your car as a container for personal belongings. Your possessions are susceptible to theft while your car is in transit and while on the docks at both ends. Many shippers and carriers will not accept your vehicle if it contains personal belongings.

If you should, against my advice, decide to leave personal property in your car, remember that the entire contents of the car must be declared to customs on entry. Failure to do so can result in a fine and seizure of the car and its contents.

Ship your personal belongings through the proper channels: the luggage shipping department of your shipping company or airline. The cost will be incidental for the peace of mind it will purchase. The money you save by placing things in your car will not justify inciting people to damage the car in attempts to steal your belongings.

A TYPICAL SHIPPING FORM • PAGE 89

If you are in Europe at the time of shipping, this should be filled out by the shipper in your presence. Otherwise, the shipper and your dealer will fill it in. Be certain to specify and check on your marine insurance.

econopak transcar

Speditionsgesellschaft mbH

Flughafen Frachtzentrum
Gebäude 458a
6000 FRANKFURT/MAIN 75
Telefon: (0611) 6902518
(0611) 691040
Telex: 4170201

EXPORT-EXCEPTION REPORT AND INVENTORY

AFFILIATED WITH OFFICES IN: MUNCHEN · GENEVE · ZÜRICH · LONDON · LIVERPOOL · BRÜSSEL · HERVE/LIEGE · BEIRUT · PARIS
NEW YORK · LOS ANGELES · HOUSTON · MIAMI

Ref. No. ....

A. We hereby certify having received the car designated below for shipment.

Owner: ....

Make and Year: ....   Model and color: ....

License No.: ....   Mileage on Speedometer: ....

Chassis No.: ....

From Receiving Location: ....   To: ....

B. The following exceptions were noted:

X	D	R	T	L	B	M	☐
SCRATCHED	DENTED	RUSTED	TORN	LOOSE	BROKEN	MISSING	Heavily dust/mud covered

(Minor deficiencies due to normal use such as hairline scratches etc. are not listed)
Defects if any not visible
Travel stained

C. Inventory		Remarks:
Spare tire	Yes — No	....
Jack & handle	Yes — No	....
Toolset	Yes — No	....
Hub caps	Yes — No	
Windshield wipers	Yes — No	Accepted: ....
Mirrors inside & outside		City Date
Safety belts front & rear	Yes — No	
Radio / Cassette	Yes — No	Received by representative of ECONOPAK TRANSCAR
Make		
Antenna	Yes — No	I herewith verify the above exceptions and I understand and accept the terms as printed on the reverse side.
Cigarette ligther	Yes — No	
Clock	Yes — No	
Extra ligths	....	....
Floor mats	Yes — No	Signature of owner or his representative Date
Car keys		full home address:
Car documents received	....	tel.:

No responsibility is accepted for any personal effects
or loose sparepart items or nonallowable items.

Such articles must be removed by owner.

For shipments from September 1st to April 15th cars must have
antifreeze protection for minus 20° Fahrenheit min.

Wir arbeiten ausschließlich auf Grund der Allgemeinen Deutschen Spediteurbedingungen (ADSp) und der Beförderungs- und Lagerbedingungen des
DeutschenMöbeltransportes, neuester Fassung. Gerichtsstand: München.

All contracts and orders are subject to the General German Forwarders Terms (Allgemeine Deutsche Spediteurbedingungen, ADSp) latest issue.

Geschäftsführer: Joachim Schweizer · HRB 68 463 Amtsgericht München.

LAMBORGHINI COUNTACH S

CHAPTER
9

ARRIVAL PROCEDURES

This chapter serves two important purposes. First, it will guide you through all the steps you will have to take when your car arrives in the United States. Second, it should refresh your memory of many of the points we have already covered.

The agent or shipping company in your home state will send you a notice of arrival. This notice will include the approximate day of arrival, an itemized account of the charges for dock handling (about $85), and some information about arrival and customs procedures. If you have neglected to do it, this notice should serve as a *final reminder to have your car insured by a domestic insurer before it arrives in the United States.* You must be sure your car is insured at *all* times.

Clearing Customs

CUSTOMS HOUSE BROKER

I recommend that both inexperienced and experienced importers use the services of a customs house broker. It will save you time and aggravation. The charge for the services of the customs house broker varies from broker to broker, but it averages about one percent of the value of the car. Your conversion center can suggest a good and reputable customs house broker.

Since you should not allow your car to sit on the docks (which invites damage), make all your arrangements with the customs house broker at least a week before your vehicle is scheduled to arrive. The customs house will do all of the following:

- Pay and clear the terminal charges (approximately $85)

- Arrange customs clearance (approximately $175)

- Pay the duty. (See chapter 14, *U.S. Customs & Duty*)

- Issue a bond for the DOT and the EPA. (See chapter 11, *DOT*, and chapter 12, *EPA*.) This bond will cost approximately 1 percent of the total value of the vehicle plus the duty to the nearest $1000. You will also be charged a bonding fee of approximately $250.

  EXAMPLE: If your car is worth $30,000:
  - The *duty* (2.7 percent) will be $810
  - The value of the *bond* is based on the value of the car ($30,000) plus the duty ($810) to the nearest $1000 ($31,000). The bond will be 1 percent of $31,000, or $310.

- Therefore, the charges the customs house will pay for you will be:

Terminal charges	$ 85
Customs clearance	175
Duty	810
Bond	310
Bonding fee	250
TOTAL	$1630

(Keep in mind that these figures are just a general guideline.)

The customs house broker will take care of all the paperwork and all other procedures to ensure that your vehicle clears customs. Clearing customs will usually take three to four days which includes the day(s) customs will spend inspecting your car.

NECESSARY DOCUMENTS

In order to have the customs house clear and bond your car, you will have to provide the following documents:

- *Customs power of attorney.* You will have to sign a limited power of attorney to have your customs house broker fill out all the customs documents, prepare the paperwork, handle your money, pay U.S. Customs charges, and pay the other handling charges.

- *Financial statement* or *irrevocable letter of credit.* These will be needed in order to establish your bond. Do not pay cash for your bond, because your money will not be released for one year for a noncommercial entry and three years for a commercial entry. U.S. Customs will not pay interest on any cash left with them.

- *Application for bond.* This will include references (friends, lawyer, accountant), with addresses, phone numbers, social security number.

- *Original bill of lading.* The shipping company will not release your vehicle to anyone—not even you—without this document. Your customs house broker will sign or stamp the bill of lading as your attorney in fact.

- A copy of the *bill of sale.* This is necessary to establish the price of the vehicle.

- A copy of the *original title.* This is necessary to prove that you are in fact the owner of the specific vehicle listed in the bill of lading.

PICKING UP YOUR CAR

After your car has cleared customs, the customs house broker may authorize your conversion center to pick up your car, or you may of course pick it up at the docks. If you should elect to pick up the car yourself, the procedure is very simple. Have your customs house broker make an appointment for you at U.S. Customs. This will usually be between 8 and 11 A.M. on a weekday. Before you go to customs itself, you will have to stop at the customs house broker. They will give you all the documents you will need to pick up the car. Among these documents will be a pick-up order. Be sure to take both your driver's license and passport (if you have one) for identification. You should expect to spend an hour or two at the customs office, depending on how busy they are. (See chapter 14, *U.S. Customs & Duty* for more details.)

If you pick up your own vehicle, it is your responsibility to note any damages on the vehicle report. Be sure to do this before signing anything. Any damage should be immediately reported to the shipping company or its representative. Call your customs house broker if you need assistance.

Often you will find that your vehicle will not start because the battery's charge is low. Always check the oil and water levels before driving your car. Make sure there is gas in the tank. (You should leave about a quarter tank of gas in the vehicle when you turn it over to the shipper in Europe.) To be on the safe side, when you pick up your car bring jumper cables, pliers, a screwdriver, and a gallon of gas.

Upon picking up your car, you are only permitted to drive the car from the pier to your residence and then on to the conversion center. Subsequently, you are permitted to drive the car to the laboratory for emission tests. Otherwise, you are not permitted to drive the car for any reason until it has satisfactorily passed all emission and safety tests and inspections, and has been registered.

Remember that you only have International Transit Plates at this point. You'll be stopped for traffic violations if you drive your car for any purpose other than to your residence or the conversion center, and, of course, to the Department of Motor Vehicles. So resist the temptation to take it out for a spin.

European registration goes out of effect once your car leaves Europe, and stateside regulations go into effect once it is approved at the Department of Motor Vehicles.

> *Your car must be registered somewhere in the United States.* You may not drive with a European transit plate registration, except for the purposes stated previously.

Registering Your Vehicle

After your vehicle has been modified and certified by the DOT and the EPA, you should go directly to the Department of Motor Vehicles in your state to register the car. *Your car must be registered somewhere in the United States.* You may not drive with a European transit plate registration, except for the purposes stated previously. Keep your international plates as a souvenir if you wish, but please don't try to drive with them.

In California a privately imported vehicle with fewer than 7,500 miles on it may not be registered. Many California residents will have to register their vehicles in other states. If you have a second home in another state, this will not be a problem. Some people will have 7,500 miles on their car from driving in Europe, or come up with legal out-of-state registrations.

What I cannot suggest or condone is advancing your speedometer. This is clearly illegal, and there is no need to even consider this when there are other legal ways to register your car with the 7,500 driven miles on it. Keep in mind that the California Department of Motor Vehicles is a wise agency; they may ask to see your service book and check out the car to ascertain if it has actually been driven. Keep your service records and gasoline receipts just in case.

REGISTRATION CHECKLIST

Below is a checklist of documents you will need and procedures you will go through to register your car. If you plan ahead you can get your car registered in a single visit to your Department of Motor Vehicles.

- Complete both sides of the application for registration (including your signature) **at the motor vehicle office.**

- Take your ownership certificate or some equivalent evidence of ownership, such as your bill of sale.

- Take your current European registration certificate (if you have one).

- Take a current smog certificate. (Most states do not require this for diesel-powered vehicles.)

- Department personnel or a peace officer will verify the vehicle identification number.

- You are supposed to surrender your international transit plates if they are current, although usually they will let you keep them if you request to do so.

- If the vehicle was a gift, fill out the statement of facts at the motor vehicles' office.

- Sales tax may be due if the vehicle was purchased out of state. (See chapter 15, *Taxes*.) Take a check.

- Take Department of Transportation importation document HS-7. (See chapter 11, *DOT*.)

- Take your driver's license, passport, or birth certificate for identification.

Just a couple of quick reminders to keep you out of trouble:

1. You may not sell or offer to sell your vehicle until the bond has been liquidated. (More on this in chapters 11 and 12.)

2. U.S. Customs will not forget you and your vehicle if you do not receive a DOT and EPA approval letter within the time limit mentioned in chapters 11 and 12.

FREIGHT BILL AND ARRIVAL NOTICE • PAGE 97

Your shipping company or their agent at the point of destination will send this notification of your vehicle's arrival date to you and/or your customs house broker. You should receive notification about a week before arrival date.

LINER BILL OF LADING • PAGE 98

A very important form with owner's name, address, type of vehicle, and chassis (identification) number. This will be included with the arrival notice.

PICK UP ORDER • PAGE 99

Either you or your customs house broker will get this form from the shipping company once you have paid the terminal charges referred to on the freight bill and arrival notice.

DOT DECLARATION FORM H.S.-7 • PAGES 100-101

U.S. Customs will complete this form at the time of pick up, and forward it to the DOT. It advises them that you have imported a vehicle under bond.

THESE CHARGES ARE PAYABLE AT _____
PRIOR TO DELIVERY OF CARGO

NOTIFY:

ALSO NOTIFY:

| B/L No.: |
| MS |
| ARRIVING ON OR ABOUT - PORT |
| PIER: |
| FOR TRANSHIPMENT TO: |
| FROM: |
| VIA: |

FREIGHT BILL AND ARRIVAL NOTICE

MARKS AND NUMBERS	NO. OF PKGS.	DESCRIPTION OF PACKAGES AND GOODS	GROSS WEIGHT	MEASUREMENT

CHARGE	WEIGHT	MEAS.	RATE	AMOUNT
			TOTAL PREPAID	✦✦✦✦✦✦✦✦✦
			TOTAL COLLECT	

| Shipper | **V.A.G TRANSPORT GMBH, Wolfsburg** | **LINER BILL OF LADING** |
| CARRIER: |

Consignee

Agent at port of Destination:

Notify address

General Average and New Jason Clause, Chamber of Shipping War Risk Clauses 1 and 2, P. & I. Club Oil Bunker Clause, GENCON Strike Clause and USA Clause Paramount form part of this Bill of Lading.

The stipulations, terms, conditions and exceptions of the contract mutually agreed between Carrier and Merchant on the
form part of and apply to this Bill of
Lading and take precedence of all other stipulations, terms, conditions and exceptions of this Bill of Lading.

84183

Pre-carriage by*	Place of receipt by pre-carrier*
Vessel	Port of loading
Port of discharge	Place of delivery by on-carrier*

| Marks and Nos | Number and kind of packages, description of goods | Gross weight kg | Measurement m³ |

Particulars furnished by the Merchant

SAMPLE

Exceptions as per corresponding Survey Report.

SHIPPED ON BOARD UNDER DECK - FREIGHT PREPAID.

It is expressly agreed that this is a shipment of a used car/cars and that signs of ordinary wear and tear such as minor stains, scratches, chips and dents which might affect the external aspect of the good is to be considered inherent to the special nature of this cargo. Acknowledgement of the receipt of this car/cars in apparent good order and condition is not a representation that such condition of minor stains, scratches, chips and dents or the like did not exist on receipt by the carrier.

SHIPPED on board in apparent good order and condition, weight, measure, marks, numbers, quality, contents and value unknown, for carriage to the Port of Discharge or so near thereunto as the Vessel may safely get and lie always afloat, to be delivered in the like good order and condition at the aforesaid Port unto Consignees or their Assigns, they paying freight as indicated here in plus other charges incurred in accordance with the provisions contained in this Bill of Lading.
In accepting this Bill of Lading the Merchant expressly accepts and agrees to all its stipulations on both pages, whether written, printed, stamped or otherwise incorporated, as fully as if they were all signed by the Merchant.
One original Bill of Lading must be surrendered duly endorsed in exchange for the goods or delivery order.
IN WITNESS whereof the Master of the said Vessel has signed the number of original Bills of Lading stated below, all of this tenor and date, one of which being accomplished, the others to stand void.

The Merchant shall pay a demurrage rate of U.S. $ per day or pro rata according to clause A of this Bill of Lading.	Place and date of issue E M D E N
* Applicable only when document used as a Through Bill of Lading	Freight payable at Wolfsburg	
	Number of original Bs/L 3/three	Signature
		for the Master and the owner **Emder Verkehrsgesellschaft AG** i.V. as agents

PICK UP ORDER/D.O.

DATE

IMPORTING CARRIER	FROM PORT OF/ORIGIN AIRPORT	OUR REF. NUMBER	ARRIVAL DATE	FREE TIME EXP

LOCATION OF MERCHANDISE

DELIVER TO →

THE CARRIER OR CARTMAN TO WHOM THIS ORDER IS ASSIGNED WILL BE RESPONSIBLE FOR ANY STORAGE AND DEMURRAGE CHARGES RESULTING FROM NEGLIGENCE.

IMPORTANT: NOTIFY US AT ONCE IF DELIVERY CANNOT BE EFFECTED AS INSTRUCTED.

BROKER/IMPORTER NAME	AUTHORIZED SIGNATURE	FREIGHT CHARGES
		☐ COD ☐ PREPAID ■ COLLECT ☐ BANK RELEASE

TRUCKING COMPANY NAME →

IS AUTHORIZED TO PICK UP THE MERCHANDISE INDICATED BELOW.

DATE & SIGNATURE OF RECEIVER	NO. PKGS. REC'D.

MARKS & NUMBERS	ENTRY NUMBER	PKGS. BY ENTRY	IMPORTING CARRIER & B/L OR AWB NO.	DESCRIPTION OF GOODS & WT

SAMPLE

THE RECEIPT OF THIS DELIVERY ORDER WILL SERVE AS A PRELIMINARY NOTICE OF INTENT TO FILE CLAIM AGAINST THE IMPORTING CARRIER FOR ANY DAMAGE TO, AND/OR LOSS OF THE SHIPMENT WITH THE UNDERSTANDING THAT THE FINAL CLAIM WILL BE MADE BY THE IMPORTER OR THEIR INSURANCE COMPANY.

PACKAGE COUNT VALIDATION

DATE_____

NO. OF PKGS.

AGENT OF DELIVERING CARRIER_____

(NAME)   (TITLE)

DELIVERED QUANTITIES VERIFIED_____

(SIGNATURE OF CUSTOMS OFFICER)   (BADGE NO.)

CUSTOMS PERMIT	PKG. NOS. HELD BY U.S. CUSTOMS TO FOLLOW	GO NO.
☐ ATTACHED ☐ LODGED WITH U.S. CUSTOMS		

DOCUMENTS ATTACHED

☐ DELIVERY ORDER ☐ ☐ DOCK RECEIPT ☐ B/L	DELIVERY CHARGES
	PER

CUSTOMER COPY

**IMPORTATION OF MOTOR VEHICLES AND MOTOR VEHICLE EQUIPMENT
SUBJECT TO FEDERAL MOTOR VEHICLE SAFETY STANDARDS**
(P.L. 89-563 SECTS. 108 AND 114, 19 C.F.R. 12.80)

FORM APPROVED
O.M.B. No. 2127-0002

This report is required by law and regulation (P.L. 89-563 and 19 C.F.R. 12.80). Failure to report will result in the refusal of entry of the vehicle(s) or equipment into the U.S.

PORT OF ENTRY	PORT CODE NUMBER	CUSTOMS ENTRY NUMBER AND DATE
IMPORT VESSEL OR CARRIER	MAKE OF MOTOR VEHICLE	
MODEL	MODEL YEAR / BODY STYLE	
CHASSIS SERIAL NUMBER	ENGINE NUMBER	

DESCRIPTION OF MERCHANDISE IF MOTOR VEHICLE EQUIPMENT RATHER THAN A MOTOR VEHICLE IS BEING ENTERED ON THIS ENTRY

I DECLARE that the motor vehicle or equipment item (merchandise hereafter) described above is being offered for importation under the provisions of Title 19, Code of Federal Regulations, Part 12.80 as indicated by the section checked below:

☐ 1. Such merchandise was manufactured on a date when there were no applicable standards in effect. (i.e., motorcycles before 1/1/69; all others before 1/1/68). (12.80(b)(1)(i))

☐ 2. Such merchandise conforms to all applicable safety standards and bears a certification label affixed by its original manufacturer in accordance with P.L. 89-563, Section 114 (15 U.S.C. 1403) and regulations issued thereunder (49 CFR Parts 555, 567 or 568). (12.80(b)(1)(ii))

☒ 3. Such merchandise was not manufactured in conformity with all applicable safety standards, but has been or will be brought into conformity with such standards as evidenced by a true and complete statement to be submitted by the importer or consignee to the Administrator, National Highway Traffic Safety Administration (NHTSA) NEF-32, within 120 days or such additional time as may be agreed to by the Administrator, NHTSA, for good cause shown, but within the time frame set forth in 19 CFR 12.80(e)(2) (copy on reverse side of this form). Such statement shall identify the manufacturer, contractor, or other person who has brought the merchandise into conformity with such standards and shall describe the exact nature and extent of the work performed. It is further declared that the merchandise will not be sold or offered for sale until the bond required for 12.80(e)(1) shall have been released. (12.80(b)(1)(iii))

☐ 4. It is intended solely for export and such merchandise and the outside of its container, if any, are so labeled. (12.80(b)(1)(iv))

☐ 5. I am a nonresident of the United States and am importing the merchandise for personal use for a period not to exceed one year from the date of entry and I will not sell it within the United States. My Passport Number is: _____
and was issued by (Country) _____
(12.80(b)(1)(v))

☐ 6. I am a member of the armed forces of a *foreign* country, or a member of the Secretariat of a public international organization and so designated under the International Organization Immunities Act (22 U.S.C. 288), as listed in 19 CFR 148.87, on assignment in the United States, or a member of the personnel of a foreign government on assignment in the United States who comes within the class of persons for whom free entry of vehicles has been authorized by the Department of State and I am importing the merchandise for purposes other than resale. A copy of my official orders to assignment within the United States is attached. (12.80(b)(1)(vi))

☐ 7. I am importing the merchandise solely for purposes of ☐ show, ☐ test, ☐ experiment, ☐ competition (for purposes of this declaration, competition vehicles are those originally manufactured or modified prior to entry for competition use only), ☐ repairs or alterations, in accordance with the attached statement which describes fully the use and final disposition to be made of the merchandise. I understand that of the above, only vehicles entered for test or experiment may be licensed or used on the public roads and then only where such use is an integral part of the test or experiment described in the attached statement in which case the vehicle may be licensed or used on the public roads for a period not to exceed one year. Such use may be made for two additional years upon application to and approval by the Administrator, NHTSA. (12.80(b)(1)(vii) (12.80(b)(2))

☐ 8. Such vehicle was not manufactured primarily for use on the public roads and is not a "motor vehicle" as defined in Section 102 of the Act (15 U.S.C. 1391). (12.80(b)(1)(viii))

☐ 9. Such vehicle is an incomplete vehicle as defined in 49 CFR Part 568. (12.80(b)(1)(ix))

PRINTED OR TYPED NAME OF IMPORTER	IMPORTER'S ADDRESS (Street, City, State, Zip Code)
PRINTED OR TYPED NAME OF DECLARANT (Legal Agent, including Customhouse Brokers)	DECLARANT'S ADDRESS (Street, City, State, Zip Code)

DECLARANT'S CAPACITY	DECLARANT'S SIGNATURE	DATE

(b) (2) A vehicle imported solely for the purpose of test or experiment which is the subject of a declaration filed under paragraph (b)(1)(vii) of this section may be licensed for use on the public roads for a period not to exceed 1 year from the date of importation if use on the public roads is an integral part of the test or experiment. The vehicle may be licensed for use on the public roads for one or more further periods which, when added to the initial 1 year period, shall not exceed a total of 3 years, upon application to and approval by the Administrator, NHTSA.

(c) Declaration; contents.

(1) Each declaration filed under paragraph (b)(1) of this section shall include the name and address in the United States of the importer or consignee, the date and the entry number (if applicable), the make, model, and engine and body serial numbers, or other identification numbers (if a vehicle), or a description of the item (if an equipment item), and shall be signed by the importer or consignee.

(2) Each declaration filed under paragraph (b)(1)(vii) of this section which relates to a vehicle or equipment item imported for the purpose of show, competition, repair, or alteration shall have attached a statement fully describing the use to be made of the vehicle or equipment item and its ultimate disposition.

(3) Each declaration filed under paragraph (b)(1)(vii) of this section which relates to a vehicle imported solely for the purpose of test or experiment shall have attached a statement fully describing the test or experiment, the estimated period of time necessary to use the vehicle on the public roads, and the disposition to be made of the vehicle after completion of the test or experiment.

(4) Any declaration filed under paragraph (b)(1) of this section may, if appropriate, relate to more than one vehicle or equipment item imported on the same entry.

(e) (2) If the bond release letter is not received by the district director within 180 days after entry, the district director shall issue a Notice of Redelivery, Customs Form 4647, requiring the redelivery to Customs custody of the vehicle or equipment item. If the vehicle or equipment item is not redelivered to Customs custody or exported under Customs supervision within the period allowed by the district director in the Notice of Redelivery, liquidated damages shall be assessed in the full amount of a bond given on Customs Form 7551. If the transaction has been charged against a bond given on Customs Form 7553 or 7595, liquidated damages shall be assessed in the amount that would have been assessed against a bond given on Customs Form 7551.

(g) Vehicle or equipment item introduced by means of a fraudulent or false declaration. Any person who enters, introduces, attempts to enter or introduce, or aids or abets the entry, introduction, or attempted entry or introduction, of a vehicle or equipment item into the Customs territory of the United States by means of a fraudulent entry declaration, or by means of a false entry declaration made without reasonable cause to believe the truth of the declaration, may incur liabilities under section 592, Tariff Act of 1930, as amended (19 U.S.C. 1592).

PART III

CONVERSION & UNITED STATES REGULATIONS

PORSCHE 930 TURBO •

CONVERTING YOUR CAR

Since vehicles privately imported to the United States from Europe do not conform to U.S. safety and emission regulations, you will undoubtedly have to convert your vehicle. Both U.S. Customs and the state in which you register your car will require that your automobile comply with the Department of Transportation's safety regulations and the Environmental Protection Agency's emission regulations.

Do It Right!

At this point, let me clarify that the EPA and the DOT are two separate government agencies which basically have nothing to do with one another. Your conversion center will be doing the work required to fulfill the separate regulations of both the EPA and DOT. For the EPA, they will be preparing your vehicle for an exacting fifteen hour Federal Test Procedure (FTP) which will demonstrate conformity to federal emission standards. For the DOT, they will develop a "picture book" to send to Washington. This is a photo series showing the work done on your vehicle to bring it into compliance with federal safety standards. But more about this in chapters 11 and 12. You will be paying your modifier one price to meet all standards.

The modifications to your car should be done by a reliable engineering center; that is to say, a firm or an individual with extensive experience modifying your type of car. These modifications are quite complex, so do not plan to make them yourself even if you have a great knowledge of mechanics. The modifications must be done with very expensive equipment using state-of-the-art parts. Unless you make your living in this field, you are not likely to have the expertise necessary. Since all the modifications will be inspected and tested by the DOT and the EPA, everything must be done correctly. More than this, some of the parts required, including electrical circuits and safety and strengthening features require custom design and fabrication.

Even the most advanced European engine will not meet strict U.S. emission standards. You will save money, time, and headaches by having your vehicle converted by the most experienced and reliable conversion center you can find in your state. Have them show you their shop and their work. Ask for references. It is very important that the work be done correctly the first time.

Your vehicle must be submitted to severe, expensive ($800 to $1500), and lengthy (almost fifteen hours) tests by the EPA. If the vehicle should fail the tests, you will have to pay the full amount to have it tested again.

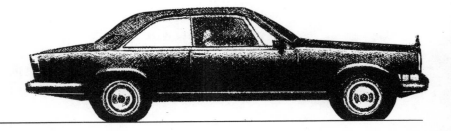

Your local EPA test lab will probably not recommend a good conversion center. However, they might be persuaded to tell you if the converter you are considering is not reliable. Don't bother to ask a factory authorized dealer for information about converters. It is hardly in his interest to help you with such a problem.

The conversion center you use should offer you assistance in bonding your vehicle (see chapter 13) and in clearing customs. If you wish, they will also pick up your car at the dock and drive it to their conversion center. If you choose — and I highly recommend that you so choose — they will also take your car to the test lab to make sure the tests are run properly. As a matter of fact, your converter and customs house broker can take care of everything from port through final testing for all U.S. regulations.

Be sure that your conversion center has good insurance to cover your vehicle while it is in its possession. Specify this in your contract with the center. Check with its insurance agency. When it comes to insurance, as I've said over and over, always check yourself, rather than relying on assurances from centers or dealers.

Insist that your converter give you a written guarantee that your vehicle will conform to both the EPA and the DOT regulations before the U.S. Customs time limit expires. If your conversion center is reliable, they will give you a written guarantee stipulating that once your vehicle is converted, it will successfully pass all EPA and DOT tests. The guarantee should specify that if the car fails the tests, your converter will bring it back to his shop, will fix what is wrong, and will take it back to the lab to be tested again — all at his own expense. Unless you receive such a written guarantee, you should take your car elsewhere.

The doors must be reinforced and modified to meet DOT standard FMVSS 206.

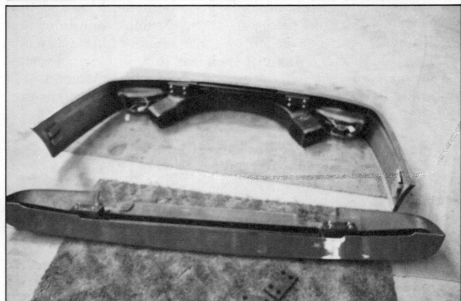

The bumpers must be reinforced according to DOT standard FMVSS 215.

A typical scene at a conversion center.

Modifications of electrical systems.

Measuring exhaust emissions for comparison to federal standards to verify compliance.

Use U.S. Conversion Centers

Do not have your vehicle converted in Europe. If, against my recommendation, you should succumb to the temptation to convert your car abroad, at least make sure the conversion center has an affiliated shop in your home state. Check with both shops to make sure they both have the same owner. Resist the temptation to convert your car abroad, though. It can only bring you grief.

For one thing, no European lab is authorized to run the EPA tests. These tests have to be performed in the United States. Although some Europeans claim to be able to perform these tests—and perhaps they can—the results are not valid. You can imagine the situation you would find yourself in if your car failed these tests and your converter had no local shop. All the work would have to be done again at your expense, and the tests would have to be run again, also at your expense.

I have said previously, and it bears repeating, that your converter should take your car to the EPA emission test (FTP). Very few people outside the field understand the highly technical testing procedures. Moreover, the labs are privately owned. Some of them, frankly, are not honest. To avoid any problems or errors and the expense and time they would cost you, a professional should accompany your car to these crucial tests.

CONVERSION COSTS

I have included a list of the prices you could normally expect to pay to have your vehicle converted. These prices are approximate and will vary from converter to converter. They include the cost of the DOT and EPA inspections and tests, the cost of your converter's guarantee, and the costs of all documents and paperwork.

The prices for conversion to meet EPA and DOT standards are always more expensive for the exotic models such as Ferrari, Jaguar, Maserati, Lamborghini and Rolls-Royce. These cars are so "specially made" that everything is very complex to replace and a lot of custom work must be done.

The exotic cars use parts that are very expensive to begin with, so replacement adds a lot to the normal conversion costs. Any electronic, electric or mechanical devices are very sensitive, and adjustment, deletion or addition of such devices will be very expensive. Also, any 12-cylinder vehicles will be much more complicated to modify.

This is why I strongly urge you to contact your conversion center or stateside modifier before you buy a special or exotic car (or for that matter any car). You need to be sure that your car can in fact be modified and what the cost will be. Needless to say, the time involved to do the work will take longer and the EPA tests will be more difficult to pass. Check references from your conversion center carefully to be sure they have had successful experience with a job such as yours.

Table 10-1

• Page 112

Table 10-1

APPROXIMATE CONVERSION COSTS TO MEET
EPA & DOT REGULATIONS

MODEL	DOT	EPA	DOT/EPA
Alfa Romeo			
All Models	2250	1750	4000
GTV Models	3200	3500	6700
Audi			
80-90-200	2650	4100	6750
Quatro	2750	4200	6950
BMW			
3	2200	1800	4000
5	2600	3200	5800
6	2500	3500	6000
7	2700	3500	6200
M635	2400	3600	6500
Ferrari			
308	3400	3600	7000
400	4400	4600	8000
Mondial	3400	3600	7000
Testa Rosa	4000	6000	10000
Jaguar			
XJ6	2400	2600	5000
12 cylinder models	4000	4500	8500
Lamborghini			
Countach LP 5000S	4000	6000	10000
Maserati			
2.5L Bi-turbo	3000	4000	7000
Kyalami Quatro-Porte	4000	5000	9000
Mercedes	From 4450 to 5000 depending on the model		
Porsche			
924/944	2400	2800	5200
911/SC-Camera Turbo	2550	2950	5200
928	2550	2950	5500
Rolls-Royce*			
All models	1950	3750	7000
Corridre Convertible	5000	7000	12000
Silver Spur	4750	6750	11500

*Make sure the Rolls-Royce
you buy is equipped
with a *solex converter*
not an S.U. converter.

Reputable Conversion Centers

The following shops are among the best conversion centers I have located in the United States as of this printing.

Fairway Environmental Engineering, Inc.
3032 Kashiwa Street
Torrance, California 90505

Telephone: (213) 775-7818
Telex: 181959

Service on every model including the Renault Turbo.

Prancing Horse Farm
2111 Emmonton Park Road
Edgewood, Maryland 21040

Telephone: (301) 679-5900

They offer complete service on all makes and models, and specialize in Ferrari.

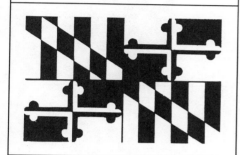

Chariots of Desire
P. O. Box 15
Plumsteadville, PA 18949

Telephone: (215) 766-0254

Primarily for Mercedes, BMW and Jaguar.

OTHER CONVERSION CENTERS
(Listed by State)

All of these conversion centers offer full service which includes bonding, shipping from Europe, picking your car up at the dock, clearing customs, duty, and complete follow through on EPA and DOT requirements. But check before you sign an agreement with them, as new management does not always continue with the good policies of the original management.

COLORADO:

Colorado Compliance Center
17757 East Crestridge Place
Aurora, Colorado 80015

Telephone: (303) 693-2226

Specialties: Jaguar, Mercedes, Lamborghini, Volkswagen, Saab, Volvo, Audi, Porsche.

FLORIDA:

Auto Safety and Emission Center, Inc.
1201 Georgia Street
Delray Beach, Florida 33444
(mailing address: 781 W. Oakland Park Blvd.,
Fort Lauderdale, Florida 33311)

Telephone: (305) 276-7103

Specialties: BMW, Porsche, Mercedes.

ILLINOIS:

Classic Motors, Inc.
P. O. Box 346
Westmount, Illinois 60559

Telephone: (312) 971-2002

Specialties: Mercedes, BMW, Porsche, Ferrari, Rolls-Royce.

Mid-West Equipment
Oak Grove, Illinois 65047

Telephone: (312) 981-0555

They offer complete service and specialize in Mercedes, BMW, Porsche, Ferrari and Jaguar.

NEW JERSEY:

Henry's Foreign Auto
451 Route 9 North
Woodbridge, New Jersey 07095

Telephone: (201) 636-7017

Specialties: Mercedes, BMW, Porsche, Ferrari, Lamborghini, Rolls-Royce.

NEW YORK:

Precision Testing Laboratories
66 Park Place
East Hampton, New York 11937

Telephone: (516) 324-0405

Specialties: Mercedes, Jaguar, Ferrari, Rolls-Royce.

Limited Edition South
715 North Highway
Hampton, New York 11968

Telephone: (516) 283-7786
(516) 283-7959

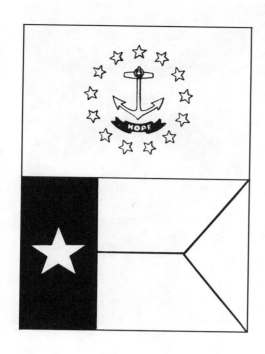

RHODE ISLAND:

Village Imports of New England, Inc.
1698 East Main Road
Portsmouth, Rhode Island 02871

Telephone: (401) 683-5120

Specialties: Mercedes, Porsche, BMW, Jaguar, Ferrari, Alfa Romeo, Lamborghini, Rolls-Royce, Honda.

TEXAS:

Professional Conversion
9205 King James Row
Dallas, Texas 75247

Telephone: (214) 631-2412

They offer complete service, and specialize in Mercedes, BMW, Porsche, Jaguar and Ferrari.

Mario's Motors
6343 Beverly Hill
Houston, Texas 77057

Telephone: (713) 780-7934

Specialties: Mercedes, BMW, Porsche, Jaguar, Ferrari, Rolls-Royce.

VERMONT:

German Imports
1900 Williston Road
So. Burlington, Vermont 05401

Telephone: (802) 658-1709

Specialties: Porsche, BMW, Mercedes

VIRGINIA:

Tyson's Motor, Inc.
P.O. Box 201
Vienna, Virginia 22180

Telephone: (703) 827-0022

Specialties: Mercedes, BMW, Porsche, Ferrari.

WASHINGTON:

Eurocar International, Inc.
10692 NE 8th Street
Bellevue, Washington 98004

Telephone: (206) 451-1611

PORSCHE DP 935

11

THE DEPARTMENT OF TRANSPORTATION

The Department of Transportation is responsible for imposing safety standards and laws regarding the safe operation of your vehicle on the streets and highways of the United States.

In September of 1966 the National Traffic and Motor Vehicle Safety Act was signed into law. This law directs the Secretary of Transportation to issue federal motor vehicle safety standards to which motor vehicle manufacturers must conform. The first such standards became effective on all vehicles manufactured on or after January 1, 1968, for sale or use in the United States with the exception of FMVSS (Federal Motor Vehicle Safety Standards) No. 209 which was effective upon issuance on March 1, 1967.

Additional standards have been added each year, and still others are in the process of being developed and issued. The standards and regulations published by the DOT under the safety act are generally intended to avoid accidents, to protect the occupants of cars, and to prevent damage to the car itself. There are about 49 standards which apply to automobiles. (A DOT summary description of these standards is reprinted in Appendix 1.) Some late-model cars manufactured for sale in Europe meet many of these safety standards. However, since many European cars do not meet these standards, and since no car meets them all, it is up to you, the importer, to prove that your vehicle complies with the law before you may drive it on U.S. roads.

COMPLIANCE WITH DOT REGULATIONS

In order to demonstrate compliance with DOT regulations the importer must:

- **Modify the vehicle by installing the parts needed to comply with safety standards.**

- **Submit a statement of compliance, Form HS-189 (see Appendix 2) supported by a picture book including 35mm photographs showing the parts of the vehicle before conversion and after conversion. The photographs should include the chassis number to prove that they were taken from the vehicle mentioned.**

- **Submit a written description of the modifications and all engineering calculations needed for the modifications.**

The best evidence of conformity with federal safety regulations is the DOT certification label. It must be affixed to the driver's side door panel when the modifications are completed and approved by the DOT. A certification label affixed to a vehicle manufactured on or after September 1, 1968, must show the date of manufacture and the vehicle identification number (V.I.N.). Below is an example of what your certification label should look like.

Modified by _____   Imported by _____
Date of Manufacture   [month]   [year]
GVWR*   GAWR**   Front: Rear:
This vehicle conforms to all applicable Federal motor vehicle safety and bumper standards in effect on the date of manufacture shown above.
Vehicle Identification Number: _____   Type_____   Passenger Car_____

*Gross Vehicle Weight Rating
**Gross Axle Weight Rating

By the time your car is in the hands of your modifier, U.S. Customs will have sent the DOT the declaration form HS-7. When the DOT receives this form, it will open a file called a P.C.I. (Preliminary Customs Investigation). DOT will then send you:

(1) a *list of FMVSS's* (Federal Motor Vehicle Safety Standards) which will apply to your vehicle and which will all have to be met by your vehicle;

(2) a *P.C.I. number* which you will have to give to your modifier and include on your statement of compliance and any other correspondence with the DOT.

When the modifications to your vehicle are complete, you and your modifier will have to fill out and sign the statement of compliance. You will send the statement of compliance (DOT Form HS-198, which is reproduced in Appendix 2) along with the picture book and any other supporting documents to the DOT in Washington, D.C. Be sure to send everything by registered mail.

U.S. Department of Transportation
National Highway Traffic Safety Administration
Director, Office of Vehicle Safety Compliance
(NEF-32, CUSH)
400 Seventh Street, SW
Washington, DC 20590

If everything is in order, the DOT will send a letter of approval to the Director of Customs responsible for the port where your vehicle entered the United States. The DOT will also send you a copy of this letter. Customs will not release your bond until both DOT and EPA have approved the modifications to your car.

Normally it will take the DOT and the EPA about three months from the time your car is approved to send Customs your letter of release.

It will usually take about one month for the DOT to accept or reject your statement of compliance. If the DOT refuses or rejects your statement of compliance, it will send you a letter with an explanation. DOT will not send a letter to your conversion center, so you will have to give them a copy of the letter. Your modifier will then have to make whatever corrections the DOT requires.

This is, of course, the reason you should go to a major conversion center as listed in this book. They do thousands of cars a year. They are professional in their work, and skilled in resolving any problems. Your car will pass the tests if it has been to a professional conversion center.

All nonconforming vehicles admitted into the United States under a cash or surety bond must be brought into conformity within 120 days unless granted an extension by the DOT. In either case conformity must be substantiated within 180 days or U.S. Customs will take enforcement action.

And, lest you think you can "get away" undiscovered, let me assure you that enforcement action is taken after the final 180 days. This will be swift—your car will be seized and very likely you will not see it again, as it will either be destroyed or shipped back to Europe. So do follow the law. Do have your car professionally converted within the legal time frame. Don't attempt to circumvent the EPA and DOT regulations.

You can begin driving your car after it has passed the EPA tests. Simply go to the Department of Motor Vehicles and take along all insurance, registration papers, as well as tax and mileage (where applicable) verification. Once you receive your state plates, you can legally drive in the United States. You don't have to wait for the release of your bond.

Any additional information can be obtained by writing or calling:

U.S. Department of Transportation
National Highway Traffic Safety Administration
Office of Vehicle Safety Compliance, NEF-32
400 Seventh Street, SW
Washington, DC 20590

Telephone: (202) 426-1693

FORM NEF-32 CUS
• PAGE 121

This is a DOT form which includes the P.C.I. (Preliminary Customs Investigation) numbers and general information about the DOT regulations. Keep track of your P.C.I. number.

LIST OF FMVSS'S
• PAGE 122

This is a DOT form specifying regulations your car must comply with in order to pass inspection. Your conversion center will take care of this.

DOT APPROVAL LETTER
• PAGE 123

This letter announces that your car has satisfactorily met all DOT requirements, and the DOT agrees to release your bond. The actual process of getting your bond released may take up to three months.

DOT REJECTION LETTER
• PAGE 124

Hopefully, you will not receive this letter stating that your vehicle does not comply with DOT safety requirements. If you do, contact your conversion center immediately and bring them this letter.

COMPLIANCE DATA EVALUATION SHEET • PAGE 125

This clearly explains why your car did not satisfy DOT requirements. Bring this with the rejection letter to your conversion center.

U.S. Department
of Transportation

**National Highway
Traffic Safety
Administration**

400 Seventh Street, S W
Washington, D C   20590

You have imported the vehicle shown on the computerized sheet, Enclosure 1.

Sections 12.80(b)(1)(iii) and 12.80(e) of Title 19, Code of Federal
Regulations, require that within 120 days of the date of entry you submit
to this office a statement substantiating that the vehicle has been brought
into conformity with all applicable Federal Motor Vehicle Safety Standards
(FMVSS); if additional time is granted, the statement must reach this
office in sufficient time to allow presentation to the District Director of
Customs of a bond release letter within 180 days from the date of entry.
For proper identification, your statement and every enclosure must include
the chassis serial number and the PCI number shown above. Your statement
must also identify the manufacturer, contractor, or other person who has
brought the vehicle into conformity and must describe the exact nature and
extent of the work performed with respect to the FMVSS which are listed on
Enclosure 1. If this statement is not submitted within the time specified
above, section 12.80(e)(2) requires that the vehicle be redelivered to the
District Director of Customs at the port of entry.

Specific guidance on the requirements of the FMVSS is given on Enclosure 2
(Form HS-189). This form does not specify the complete or detailed
requirements of the FMVSS, but only indicates the areas of apparent
noncompliance which normally exist on motor vehicles not manufactured for
the U.S. market. We advise that you consult the manufacturer's
representative in the United States before attempting to bring your vehicle
into conformity, particularly if you have imported a model or type which
the manufacturer does not sell in the United States. You should note that
for some requirements dealing with crash survivability, specifically FMVSS
Nos. 203, 204, 207, 208, 210, 214, 216, 219, and 301, where applicable,
(see Enclosure 1), proof of conformance is difficult to achieve without the
manufacturer's compliance statement and in the event that you are unable to
substantiate conformance, this agency will press for redelivery and export
of the vehicle.

Upon review of your statement, the National Highway Traffic Safety
Administration may wish to verify its accuracy by requiring you to make
your vehicle available for an inspection to insure that it has, in fact,
been brought into conformity with all applicable FMVSS and that you have
not violated the National Traffic and Motor Vehicle Safety Act of 1966
(15 U.S.C. 1381 et seq.).

Failure to substantiate that the vehicle has been brought into conformity
within the allowed time renders you liable for imposition of a civil
penalty of up to $1,000 and/or assessment of liquidated damages in the
amount of the value of the vehicle, pursuant to the entry bond required by
section 12.80(e). You are also reminded that under section
12.80(b)(1)(iii) you may not sell the vehicle or offer it for sale prior to
release of the bond.

Sincerely,

Francis Armstrong
Director
Office of Vehicle Safety Compliance
Enforcement

Enclosures

Dec-20 1984   STATUS: PCI:
                      Suspense Date:

                      Port Code   :
                      Date of Deal   :   Date Tech:
                      Cus. Entry No. :   Box No:

                                                       Effective
                                                       Date of
Make   Model No.   Serial No. FMVSS

SAMPLE   CAR:

Number   Description

101   CONTROL LOCATION, IDENTIFICATION, AND ILLUMINATION
102   TRANS. SHIFT LEVER SEQ., STARTER INTERLOCK, AND TRANS. BRAKING
103   WINDSHIELD DEFROSTING AND DEFOGGING SYSTEMS
104   WINDSHIELD WIPING AND WASHING SYSTEM
105   HYDRAULIC SERV. BRK., EMERGENCY BRK., AND PARKING BRK. SYSTEMS
106   BRAKE HOSES
107   REFLECTING SURFACES
108   LAMPS, REFLECTIVE DEVICES, AND ASSOCIATED EQUIPMENT
109   NEW PNEUMATIC TIRES
110   TIRE SELECTION AND RIMS
111   REARVIEW MIRRORS
112   HEADLAMP CONCEALMENT DEVICES
113   HOOD LATCH SYSTEMS
114   THEFT PROTECTION
115   VEHICLE IDENTIFICATION NUMBER
116   MOTOR VEHICLE BRAKE FLUIDS
118   POWER OPERATED WINDOW SYSTEMS
124   ACCELERATOR CONTROL SYSTEMS
201   OCCUPANT PROTECTION IN INTERIOR IMPACT
202   HEAD RESTRAINTS
203   IMPACT PROTECTION FOR THE DRIVER FROM THE STEERING CONTROL SYSTEM
204   STEERING CONTROL REARWARD DISPLACEMENT
205   GLAZING MATERIALS
206   DOOR LOCK AND DOOR RETENTION COMPONENTS
207   SEATING SYSTEMS
208   OCCUPANT CRASH PROTECTION
209   SEAT BELT ASSEMBLIES
210   SEAT BELT ASSEMBLY ANCHORAGES
211   WHEEL NUTS, WHEEL DISCS, AND HUB CAPS
212   WINDSHIELD MOUNTING
214   SIDE DOOR STRENGTH
216   ROOF CRUSH RESISTANCE
219   WINDSHIELD ZONE INTRUSION
301   FUEL SYSTEM INTEGRITY
302   FLAMMABILITY OF INTERIOR MATERIALS
581   BUMPER STANDARD

US Department
of Transportation

National Highway
Traffic Safety
Administration

400 Seventh St. S.W.
Washington, DC 20590

18 March 1985
In Reply Refer To:
NEF-32-CUS
PCI NO.

District Director of Customs
Attn:

Dear Sir:

The National Highway Traffic Safety Administration (NHTSA) acknowledges receipt of a statement of compliance submitted by the importer for the below identified vehicle imported on Customs entry shown:

Importer's Name:
Customs Entry No. & Date:
Port Code:
Vehicle Make & Model:
Vehicle Identification No. (VIN):

The statement meets the requirements of 19 CFR 12.80(e). Release from all liability under the bond posted with respect to compliance with the requirements of NHTSA is, therefore, satisfactory. Release must be obtained from the Environmental Protection agency (EPA) relative to compliance with the emission control requirements (19 CFR 12.73), if applicable.

It should be noted that this bond release letter does not constitute agreement by NHTSA that the vehicle, in fact, is in conformance with all applicable Federal Motor Vehicle Safety Standards (FMVSS) since actual conformance is determinable only by compliance testing.

By copy of this letter the importer is advised that NHTSA reserves the right to make an actual compliance inspection of the vehicle at a future date to verify the accuracy of data contained in this statement of compliance.

Sincerely

Francis Armstrong
Director
Office of Vehicle Safety Compliance
Enforcement

CC:

U.S. Department
of Transportation

**National Highway
Traffic Safety
Administration**

400 Seventh Street, S W
Washington, D C   20590

NEF-32EBu
PCI No. Overleaf

Dear Importer:

This is in reference to your recent submission of compliance data for the
vehicle identified on the Compliance Data Evaluation Sheet (overleaf).

Your file cannot be processed because the data you submitted are insufficient to establish conformance of the vehicle, as indicated. It appears
that you are not following instructions for proper documentation of compliance as shown on page 1 of Form HS-189, and the Safety Compliance Information Sheet, both previously furnished.

Your immediate attention to this matter is required.

Sincerely,

Francis Armstrong
Director
Office of Vehicle Safety Compliance
Enforcement

cc:

U.S. Department of Transportation

National Highway Traffic Safety Administration

DEPARTMENT OF TRANSPORTATION
NATIONAL HIGHWAY TRAFFIC SAFETY ADMINISTRATION

COMPLIANCE DATA EVALUATION SHEET _____

Date _____

Importer _____ PCI # _____

Make _____ VIN _____

CE#/Date _____ FMVSS Date _____ Veh. Type _____

Review of compliance data on file for the referenced vehicle revealed insufficient documentation to establish conformance with the Federal Motor Vehicle Safety Standards (FMVSS) checked below:

FMVSS
101---CONTROL LOCATION, IDENTIFICATION, AND ILLUMINATION
( ) Controls and/or internal displays not identified with required words and/or symbols.
( ) Control and/or internal display identification not illuminated.
( ) Control ID illumination not variable.
102---TRANSMISSION SHIFT LEVER SEQUENCE, STARTER INTERLOCK, AND TRANSMISSION BRAKING EFFECT
( ) No shift pattern in view of driver.
103---WINDSHIELD DEFROSTING AND DEFOGGING SYSTEMS
( ) No defroster in vehicle.
104---WINDSHIELD WIPING AND WASHING SYSTEMS
( ) No two-speed windshield wiper system.
105---HYDRAULIC BRAKE SYSTEM
( ) No dual-circuit brake master cylinder.
( ) No brake failure warning system.
( ) Hydraulic brake fluid reservoir without informatory inscription.
106---BRAKE HOSES
( ) No required markings.
107---REFLECTING SURFACES
( ) Bright chrome wiper arms & blades, horn ring, inside rearview mirror bracket.
108---LAMPS, REFLECTIVE DEVICES, AND ASSOCIATED EQUIPMENT
( ) Nonconforming headlamps.
( ) Nonconforming headlamp housings.
( ) No parking lamps.
( ) Parking lights not on with headlamps.
( ) No sidemarker reflectors or lights.
( ) Sidemarkers of improper color.
( ) No hazard warning system.
( ) No turn signal lights.
109---NEW PNEUMATIC TIRES (Tires other than retreads, for passenger cars only)
( ) Tires without DOT symbol.
110---TIRE SELECTION AND RIMS
( ) No tire information placard.
( ) Placard with incorrect data.
111---REARVIEW MIRRORS
( ) Required mirrors not of unit magnification: L/H ( ), R/H ( ), inside ( ).
( ) Outside mirror without driver's reach.
112---HEADLAMP CONCEALMENT DEVICES
( ) Non-U.S. model configuration.

FMVSS
113---HOOD LATCH SYSTEMS
( ) No secondary hood retaining system.
114---THEFT PROTECTION
( ) No steering lock.
( ) Key removable with lock unlocked.
( ) No key warning system.
115---VEHICLE IDENTIFICATION NUMBER (VIN)
( ) No VIN plate readable from outside veh.
( ) VIN plate not permanently affixed.
118---POWER-OPERATED WINDOW SYSTEMS
( ) Non-U.S. model configuration.
119---NEW PNEUMATIC TIRES FOR VEHICLES OTHER THAN PASS. CARS (Other than retreads)
( ) Tires without valid ID number.
( ) Tires without DOT symbol.
120---TIRE SELECTION AND RIMS FOR MOTOR VEHICLES OTHER THAN PASSENGER CARS
( ) Rims without DOT symbol.
( ) No tire/rim choice information label.
121---AIR BRAKE SYSTEMS
( ) Non-U.S. model air brake system.
122---MOTORCYCLE BRAKE SYSTEMS
( ) Non-U.S. model brake system.
123---MOTORCYCLE CONTROLS AND DISPLAYS
( ) Non-U.S. model controls and displays.
124---ACCELERATOR CONTROL SYSTEMS
( ) Non-U.S. model accelerator controls.
201---OCCUPANT PROTECTION IN INTERIOR IMPACT
( ) Instrument panel not energy-absorbing.
202---HEAD RESTRAINTS
( ) No head restraints.
( ) Non-U.S. model head restraints.
203 ● IMPACT PROTECTION FOR THE DRIVER FROM STEERING CONTROL SYSTEM
( ) Steering wheel not energy-absorbing.
204 ● STEERING CONTROL REARWARD DISPLACEMENT
( ) Steering column not energy-absorbing.
205---GLAZING MATERIALS
( ) Windshield not marked AS-1.
206---DOOR LOCK & DOOR RETENTION COMPONENTS
( ) Door handle overrides rear door lock.
( ) No means for unlocking rear door from inside the vehicle.
207 ● SEATING SYSTEMS
( ) No seatback locks in both front seats.
208 - OCCUPANT CRASH PROTECTION
( ) ___ front belts missing / nonconforming.
( ) ___ rear belts missing / nonconforming.
( ) No U.S.-type seat belt warning system.
209 - SEAT BELT ASSEMBLIES
( ) Required markings not on seat belts.

FMVSS
210 ● SEAT BELT ASSEMBLY ANCHORAGES
( ) ___ anchorages missing / nonconforming.
211 - WHEEL NUTS, WHEEL DISCS, AND HUB CAPS
( ) Wheel nuts with winged projections.
212 - WINDSHIELD MOUNTING
( ) Windshield not in conforming moulding.
( ) Windshield not in retention adhesive.
214 ● SIDE DOOR STRENGTH
( ) Door beams not installed in all doors.
( ) Nonconforming door beam modification.
215 - EXTERIOR PROTECTION (9-72 thru 8-78)
( ) Bumpers not modified.
( ) Nonconforming bumper modification.
216 ● ROOF CRUSH RESISTANCE
( ) No backup for non-U.S. body design.
219 ● WINDSHIELD ZONE INTRUSION
( ) No backup for non-U.S. body design.
301 ● FUEL SYSTEM INTEGRITY
( ) No backup for non-U.S. body design.
302 - FLAMMABILITY OF INTERIOR MATERIALS
( ) No backup for non-U.S. interior mat.
PART 581 - BUMPER STANDARD (From 9-78 on)
( ) Bumpers not modified.
( ) Nonconforming bumper modification.
PART 567 - CERTIFICATION
( ) No sample of actual label furnished.
( ) Label removable without destruction.
( ) Lettering not of proper contrast.
( ) Vehicle manufacturer's name incorrect.
( ) Mo/Yr of manufacture incorrect.
( ) Weight ratings incorrect.
( ) Improper format and order of data.
( ) Bumper certification not in text.

___ Form HS-189 not signed.
___ Form HS-189 signed by an unidentified person.
___ Entry made in the name of a company, but signature not authenticated by corporate seal or notarized statement identifying the officer of the company legally able to sign the statement of compliance for the company.
___ Notarized power-of-attorney from the importer, delegating signature authority, not submitted.
___ Backup data insufficient to establish conformance, as indicated above (T= text, P= photographs).
___ Text pages and/or photographs do not show vehicle identification no. (VIN)
___ Text & photographs not cross-referenced.

MERCEDES-BENZ 500 SEL CUSTOM CONVERTIBLE •

THE ENVIRONMENTAL PROTECTION AGENCY

Under the provisions of the Clean Air Act, the Environmental Protection Agency is responsible for preserving the environment. The EPA is very strict—and should be—especially in big cities where smog and other pollution are a part of what we all breathe every day.

The Clean Air Act requires that every motor vehicle imported into the United States comply with the emission requirements applicable to the model year in which the vehicle was manufactured. Emission requirements are applicable to the 1968 and later model year gasoline-fueled vehicles, and, 1975 and later model year diesel-fueled vehicles. A manufacturer's model year usually begins during the late summer or early autumn of the previous calendar year. For example, a vehicle manufactured in September, 1977, would be a 1978 model.

Motorcycles manufactured after December 31, 1977, and gasoline-fueled and diesel-fueled engines manufactured after January 1, 1970 for use in heavy-duty vehicles must meet federal emission requirements. If a pre-1968 model car is being imported and the engine has been replaced, emission control standards must be met. Beginning with the 1971 models, fuel evaporation emission standards must be met. All vehicles produced during or after 1976 are subject to EPA catalyst retrofit requirements.

The Clean Air Act will not allow you to import a nonconforming vehicle into the United States without posting a bond with U.S. Customs equal to the value of your vehicle plus duty. Usually an importer has 90 days to bring his vehicle into compliance with EPA standards. U.S. Customs will normally wait 180 days before it will enforce this statute. "Enforcement" can mean your car will be destroyed or exported and you will be assessed financial penalties, so this is something you must tend to immediately. (See chapter 13, *Bonding Your Car*.)

THE CLEAN AIR ACT

EPA WAIVER

There are few exceptions to this rule. There is a one-time-only exemption called an *EPA Waiver* for which an individual who has never before imported a nonconforming vehicle might be eligible. The exemption means the car will not have to be brought into conformity with U.S. emission requirements for the EPA (it still must meet DOT requirements). The hitch is that the exempt vehicle must be at least five model years old at the time of importation. Also, the vehicle cannot be sold for two years unless it is first brought into conformity. One need not apply for this waiver. It will be granted automatically. Since this waiver does not apply to the DOT, your car will still have to enter the United States under a bond. The District Director of Customs will be informed of your exemption by letter from the EPA. It will usually take about 90 days after receipt of this letter for customs to release your bond. The bad news for a large number of importers is that this exemption does not apply in the state of California. Moreover, other states are considering following California's lead in refusing to grant this exemption.

Modifications for EPA

When your car clears customs, the customs office will send the EPA declaration form 3520-1. The EPA will then send you a list of the regulations applying to nonconforming imported vehicles.

Modification of a nonconforming vehicle consists of replacing, adding, or deleting the appropriate components to make the vehicle's emission equipment substantially the same as the ones imported by the manufacturer, or demonstrating conformity with the emissions standards by successful completion of the Federal Test Procedure (F.T.P.). Transforming your automobile into a virtual copy of the manufacturers' authorized imports is impractical because of the enormous cost and the fact that the U.S. representatives of the manufacturers are reluctant to assist you. Without a compliance statement from one of these representatives, there is no way to gain exact U.S. data for modification and submission.

The only solution is to have your vehicle modified by a commercial conversion center. After the modifications have been completed, conformity must be demonstrated by successfully passing the Federal Test Procedure at an acceptable laboratory. I have included a list of reputable laboratories for the F.T.P. tests, and although the EPA will not recommend labs, they will inform you of those which don't meet necessary standards. Appendix 5 shows a sample of F.T.P. test results.

The Clean Air Act emissions standards apply to the following emissions: NOx (oxides of nitrogen), HC (hydrocarbons), CO (carbon monoxide), and EHC (evaporative hydrocarbon emissions). (See Appendix 4 for EPA federal emissions standards and Appendix 6 for the EPA motor vehicle emissions test report form.)

The equipment your modifier will install on your car will, of course, depend on the size of the engine, the make and model of car, the year of the car, and the fuel induction system (carburation or fuel injection). Some typical emission control equipment involved in modifying a late-model gasoline vehicle is:

- **Catalytic converter**
- **Air pump**
- **Oxygen sensor**
- **Electronic control unit**
- **Exhaust gas recirculation system**
- **Charcoal cannister**
- **Temperature sensor, wiring and hoses**
- **Fuel filler restrictor**

The EPA tests will last almost 15 hours and will cost from $800 to $1500. Appendix 6 reproduces a report of the information the tests will generate. This report will be sent to the EPA along with 35mm photographs of the emission control equipment which has been installed. A notary public must witness the signature of the test lab officer who signs the report.

If the test results are acceptable, you and U.S. Customs will be notified by letter. If the results are not acceptable, an explicit letter detailing the causes of rejection will be sent to you. Have your modifier immediately resolve the problems. A good modifier will see your vehicle through to final approval, so this shouldn't be a problem if you have chosen carefully to begin with. That is why I recommend that your agreement state that the conversion center guarantee its work through final EPA approval.

Remember, you are under U.S. Customs time constraints, too. Don't count on getting an extension. Plan on completing your work for EPA in 90 days and for DOT in 120 days.

If you need additional information call or write the EPA.

Investigation/Imports Section
Manufacturers Operations Division (EN-340)
U.S. Environmental Protection Agency
401 M Street, S.W.
Washington, DC 20460

Telephone: (202) 382-2504

EPA Test Laboratories

Here is a partial list of reliable laboratories suggested (not recommended) by the EPA. These laboratories are able to conduct the EPA tests in accordance with the standards set for the Federal Test Procedures at this time. While the EPA does not approve or recommend labs, you might want to check with them about a specific laboratory's reliability. There are many new labs—some very good to be sure—but you need to know their record. Remember, too, lab standards change under new or different management, so find out as much as you can before committing to a test lab's services.

State emission checks (including California) or emission checks done at service stations or repair shops are not acceptable by the EPA.

Automated Custom Systems, Inc.
645 Lunt Avenue
Elk Grove Village, Illinois 60007

Telephone: (312) 952-1790

Automotive Compliance Center, Inc.
4028 N.E. 6th Avenue
Fort Lauderdale, Florida 33334

Telephone: (305) 564-8993

Automotive Compliance Laboratory, Inc.
501 Tonnelle Avenue
North Bergen, New Jersey 07047

Telephone: (201) 865-3231

Automotive Research, Inc.
1331 Upland, #E
Houston, Texas 77043

Telephone: (713) 984-1502

Automotive Testing Laboratories, Inc.
P. O. Box 289
East Liberty, Ohio 43319

Telephone: (513) 666-4351

Bendix
Advanced Products Division
900 West Maple Road
P. O. Box 2602
Troy, Michigan 48084

Telephone: (313) 362-1800

Custom Engineering
Performance and Emissions Laboratories
7091-A Belgrave Avenue
Garden Grove, California 92641

Telephone: (714) 891-5704

EG&G Automotive Research, Inc.
5404 Bandera Road
San Antonio, Texas 78238

Telephone: (512) 684-2310

Emissions Technology, Inc.
1600 Fayette Street
Conshohocken, Pennsylvania 19428

Telephone: (215) 825-7547

Ethyl Corporation
1600 West Eight Mile Road
Ferndale, Michigan 48220

Telephone: (313) 399-9600

Fairway Environmental Engineering
3032 Kashiwa Street
Torrance, California 90505

Telephone: (213) 775-7618

F. C. I. International Testing Laboratories
3132 West Adams
Santa Ana, California 92704

Telephone: (714) 754-6424

Import Certification Laboratories
421 E. Cerritos Avenue
Anaheim, California 92805

Telephone: (714) 553-0780 or 0781

Mardikian Engineering
1220 Brittmoore
Houston, Texas 77043

Telephone: (713) 468-3733

*New York City Department of Environmental Protection
Mobile Source Controls Division
75 Frost Street
Brooklyn, New York 11211

Telephone: (212) 388-4994

*Olson Engineering, Inc.
15442 Chemical Lane
Huntington Beach, California 92649

Telephone: (714) 891-4821

Satra Automotive Emissions Laboratory, Inc.
U.S. 1 and 9 South
Newark, New Jersey 07114

Telephone: (201) 242-7665

*Scott Environmental Technology, Inc.
Route 611
Plumsteadville, Pennsylvania 18949

Telephone: (215) 766-8861

*Southwest Research Institute
6220 Culebra Road
San Antonio, Texas 78284

Telephone: (512) 684-5111, ext. 2653

Vehicle Emissions and Fuel Economy Laboratory
Texas Transportation Institute
Texas A and M University
College Station, Texas 77843

Telephone: (713) 845-6176
*Also capable of testing diesel-powered vehicles

EPA WAIVER
• PAGE 133

The EPA waiver announces that your vehicle is exempt from EPA modifications and tests. Remember that your vehicle must still comply with DOT regulations and approval.

When you pick up your car, U.S. Customs will tell you how to apply for this exemption.

EPA DECLARATION FORM 3520-1 • PAGES 134–135

U.S. Customs will send this form to the EPA certifying the arrival of your vehicle, at the time you pick your vehicle up. The EPA then opens a file on your vehicle.

EPA APPROVAL LETTER
• PAGE 136

This all-important letter confirms the acceptance of your EPA test results, and releases your EPA bond.

EPA REJECTION LETTER
• PAGE 137

If you receive this letter, contact your modifier and bring a copy of this letter.

UNITED STATES ENVIRONMENTAL PROTECTION AGENCY
WASHINGTON, D.C. 20460

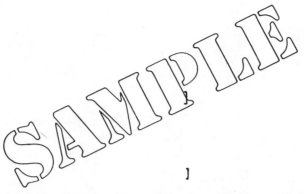

**OFFICE OF
AIR, NOISE AND RADIATION**

[   ]

[   ]

    Approval is hereby given for release of the U. S. Environmental Protection Agency (EPA) obligation on the bond for the <u>1978 or earlier model year vehicle</u> described on the attached EPA Form 3520-1. While we lack sufficient information to determine whether this vehicle has been brought into conformity with Federal emission requirements, because of the age of the vehicle at the time of importation we recommend release of the EPA obligation on the bond. Please note that this does not release the importer of the obligation to comply with Federal safety requirements administered by the U. S. Department of Transportation.

    We appreciate your cooperation in the enforcement of the joint Customs-EPA regulations.

               Sincerely yours,

               Gerard C. Kraus, Chief
               Investigation/Imports Section
               Manufacturers Operations Division
               (EN-340F)

Attachment

cc: Importer

<u>Note to Importer</u>: Because of the age of your vehicle at the time of importation, we are releasing you of the obligation to bring your vehicle into conformity with Federal emission requirements. <u>However, you still must comply with Federal safety requirements and any applicable state or local emission-related requirements</u>. Further, this determination applies only to a first-time importation of a nonconforming vehicle by an individual for personal use. It would not apply to any subsequent vehicle imported by you or to any importation for resale. <u>This is an important document. Please keep a copy of it with your vehicle registration at all times.</u>

U.S. ENVIRONMENTAL PROTECTION AGENCY

IMPORTATION OF MOTOR VEHICLES AND MOTOR VEHICLE ENGINES SUBJECT TO FEDERAL AIR POLLUTION CONTROL REGULATIONS

(Read instructions on reverse side before completing form.)

WARNING

Any person who knowingly makes a false declaration shall be fined not more than $10.000 or imprisoned not more than 5 years, or both. 18 U.S.C. 1001.

PORT OF ENTRY	DATE OF ENTRY	ENTRY NO. *(if applicable)*

IMPORT VESSEL OR CARRIER	MAKE OF VEHICLE *(or engine, if not chassis mounted or if mounted in heavy-duty vehicle)*	MODEL OF VEHICLE *(or engine. if not chassis mounted or if mounted in heavy-duty vehicle)*

MODEL YEAR OF VEHICLE *(or engine, if not chassis mounted or if mounted in heavy-duty vehicle)*	VEHICLE IDENTIFICATION NUMBER	ENGINE SERIAL NUMBER *(if not chassis mounted or if mounted in heavy-duty vehicle)*

WITH REGARD TO THE IMPORTATION OF THE DESCRIBED MOTOR VEHICLE OR MOTOR VEHICLE ENGINE, I DECLARE THAT:

1. SUCH 1971 OR SUBSEQUENT MODEL YEAR MOTOR VEHICLE OR MOTOR VEHICLE ENGINE IS COVERED BY A CERTIFICATE OF CONFORMITY ISSUED BY THE DEPARTMENT OF HEALTH, EDUCATION, AND WELFARE OR BY THE U.S. ENVIRONMENTAL PROTECTION AGENCY, AND BEARS A CERTIFICATION LABEL OR TAG.

2. SUCH 1968, 1969 OR 1970 MODEL YEAR MOTOR VEHICLE OR MOTOR VEHICLE ENGINE IS COVERED BY A CERTIFICATE OF CONFORMITY ISSUED BY THE DEPARTMENT OF HEALTH, EDUCATION, AND WELFARE OR THE U.S. ENVIRONMENTAL PROTECTION AGENCY.

WITH REGARD TO THE IMPORTATION OF THE DESCRIBED MOTOR VEHICLE OR ENGINE, I DECLARE THAT SUCH VEHICLE OR ENGINE IS <u>NOT COVERED BY A CERTIFICATE OF CONFORMITY</u> ISSUED BY THE DEPARTMENT OF HEALTH, EDUCATION, AND WELFARE OR THE U.S. ENVIRONMENTAL PROTECTION AGENCY, BUT IS ELIGIBLE FOR ADMISSION INTO THE UNITED STATES BECAUSE:

3. THE VEHICLE OR ENGINE IS BEING IMPORTED SOLELY FOR PURPOSES OF DISPLAY AND WILL NOT BE SOLD OR OPERATED ON THE PUBLIC HIGHWAYS.

4. THE IMPORTER OR CONSIGNEE IS A MEMBER OF THE ARMED FORCES OF A <u>FOREIGN COUNTRY</u>, OR MEMBER OF THE SECRETARIAT OF A PUBLIC INTERNATIONAL ORGANIZATION SO DESIGNATED PURSUANT TO 50 STAT. 669 *(22 U.S.C. 288(b))* OR A MEMBER OF THE PERSONNEL OF A FOREIGN GOVERNMENT ON ASSIGNMENT IN THE UNITED STATES WHO COMES WITHIN THE CLASS OF PERSONS FOR WHOM FREE ENTRY OF VEHICLES HAS BEEN AUTHORIZED BY THE DEPARTMENT OF STATE AND THE VEHICLE OR ENGINE WILL NOT BE SOLD IN THE UNITED STATES.

5. THE IMPORTER OR CONSIGNEE IS A <u>NON-RESIDENT OF THE UNITED STATES</u> IMPORTING SUCH VEHICLE OR ENGINE FOR PERSONAL USE FOR NOT MORE THAN ONE YEAR FROM THE DATE OF ENTRY, AND THE VEHICLE OR ENGINE WILL NOT BE SOLD IN THE UNITED STATES.

6. THE VEHICLE OR ENGINE IS BEING IMPORTED FOR THE PURPOSE OF TESTING AND WILL NOT BE SOLD OR OPERATED ON THE PUBLIC HIGHWAYS WITHOUT THE PRIOR WRITTEN CONSENT OF THE ADMINISTRATOR OF THE U.S. ENVIRONMENTAL PROTECTION AGENCY.

7. THE VEHICLE OR ENGINE IS INTENDED SOLELY FOR EXPORT.

8. THE VEHICLE OR ENGINE <u>IS NOT SUBJECT TO THE REGULATIONS UNDER THE CLEAN AIR ACT</u> BECAUSE IT IS A:

   a. VEHICLE MANUFACTURED BEFORE THE 1968 MODEL YEAR.

   b. NON-CHASSIS MOUNTED ENGINE TO BE USED IN A LIGHT-DUTY VEHICLE.
   (NOTE: A light-duty vehicle is a vehicle designed primarily for transportation of property and rated at 6,000 pounds GVW or less or designed primarily for transportation of persons with a capacity of 12 persons or less.)

   c. ENGINE MANUFACTURED BEFORE JANUARY 1, 1970 FOR USE IN A HEAVY-DUTY VEHICLE.
   (NOTE: A heavy-duty vehicle is a vehicle designed primarily for transportation of property and rated at more than 6,000 pounds GVW or designed primarily for transportation of persons with a capacity of more than 12 persons.)

   d. LIGHT-DUTY NON-GASOLINE FUELED VEHICLE. *(if diesel-fueled, only for 1974 and earlier models)*

   e. MOTORCYCLE MANUFACTURED BEFORE JANUARY 1, 1978.

   f. RACING VEHICLE NOT TO BE OPERATED ON PUBLIC STREETS OR HIGHWAYS.

9. THE VEHICLE OR ENGINE IS ONE OF A CLASS OF VEHICLES OR ENGINES FOR WHICH AN APPLICATION FOR A CERTIFICATE OF CONFORMITY IS PENDING BEFORE THE ADMINISTRATOR OF THE U.S. ENVIRONMENTAL PROTECTION AGENCY, AND IS <u>BEING IMPORTED UNDER BOND</u>.

X 10. THE VEHICLE OR ENGINE IS NOT IN CONFORMITY WITH APPLICABLE EMISSION STANDARDS, BUT WILL BE BROUGHT INTO CONFORMITY WITH SUCH STANDARDS, AND IS <u>BEING IMPORTED UNDER BOND</u>.

11. NEITHER THE IMPORTER NOR THE ULTIMATE CONSIGNEE POSSESSES SUFFICIENT INFORMATION TO MAKE ANY OF THE PRECEDING DECLARATIONS, BUT THE IMPORTER OR ULTIMATE CONSIGNEE WILL SEEK TO DETERMINE SUCH INFORMATION, AND THE VEHICLE OR ENGINE IS <u>BEING IMPORTED UNDER BOND</u>.

WARNING: Entry under provisions 9, 10, and 11 requires posting of bond at the time of entry equal to the value of the merchandise plus duty for delivery of a conformity statement no later than 90 days after entry to the District Director of Customs. <u>Written notice that a vehicle or engine has been admitted under bond must be sent by the importer not later than 5 days after entry to the U.S. Environmental Protection Agency, Manufacturers Operations Division (EN-340), Washington, D.C. 20460.</u> The information required in such notice is set forth in the instructions printed below on this form. A vehicle admitted under bond must be redelivered to port of entry unless certification is granted, or the Administrator makes a determination in writing that the vehicle has been modified to conform to applicable standards.

NAME OF IMPORTER *(Please print)*	NAME OF CONSIGNEE *(Please print)*

ADDRESS OF IMPORTER	ADDRESS OF CONSIGNEE

SIGNATURE OF IMPORTER OR CONSIGNEE

EPA Form 3520-1 (Rev. 3-81)   EDITION OF 5-80 MAY BE USED.

This form is required by law (*42 U.S.C. 1857f-2, 1857g; 19 C.F.R. 12.73*). Failure to declare a motor vehicle or motor vehicle engine can result in a fine up to the amount of $10,000 per vehicle or engine (*42 U.S.C. 1857f-4*).

INSTRUCTIONS

This form is used to determine whether a motor vehicle or motor vehicle engine can be imported into the United States.

This form must be filled out for all motor vehicles and motor vehicle engines which are imported into the United States. If there is more than one vehicle or engine in an entry, only one form needs to be filled out, provided the information on the make, model, model year and vehicle identification or engine serial numbers are provided for each vehicle or engine on an attached sheet.

SPECIAL INSTRUCTIONS FOR ITEMS 9, 10, and 11

Item

9   <u>Admission Pending Certification.</u> A vehicle or engine imported under a declaration that it is one of a class of vehicles or engines represented by test vehicles or engines for which an application for certification of conformity is pending before the U.S. Environmental Protection Agency may be conditionally admitted into the United States under bond, but will be denied final admission unless the importer or consignee follows these instructions:

1. The importer or consignee must submit to the Administrator within 5 days following conditional admission a written request that the vehicle be conditionally admitted pending certification. The written request must:

    a. Identify the test vehicle or engine which represents the vehicle or engine offered for importation.

    b. Identify the place where the vehicle or engine will be stored while the application for certification is pending before the Administrator. (See storage requirement below)

    c. Acknowledge responsibility for custody of the vehicle while certification is pending.

The certificate of conformity must be issued by the U.S. Environmental Protection Agency before the vehicle or engine may be granted final admission.

Reference: 40 C.F.R. §85.1503

10   <u>Admission Pending Modification.</u> A vehicle or engine imported under a declaration that it is not covered by a certificate of conformity, but that it will be brought into conformity with standards may be conditionally admitted into the United States under bond, but will be denied final admission unless the importer or consignee follows these instructions:

1. The importer or consignee must submit to the U.S. Environmental Protection Agency within 5 days following conditional admission a written request that he be permitted to modify the vehicle or engine so that it will be in conformity with applicable emission standards. The written request must:

    a. Specify the modifications necessary to bring the vehicle or engine into conformity with a test vehicle or engine for which a certificate of conformity has been granted. (NOTE: It is the importer's responsibility to determine from the manufacturer of the vehicle or engine to be imported what modifications are necessary.)

    b. Specify the date by which the necessary modifications will be made.

    c. Identify the place where the vehicle or engine will be stored until the U.S. Environmental Protection Agency determines that it has been brought into conformity with emission standards. (See storage requirements below.)

    d. Acknowledge responsibility for custody of the vehicle or engine while the modifications are being made and a determination of conformity is pending.

    e. Authorize representatives of the U.S. Environmental Protection Agency to inspect or test the vehicle or engine at any reasonable time in order to make a determination of conformity.

2. The importer or consignee must obtain the written determination of the U.S. Environmental Protection Agency that the vehicle or engine has been modified to conform to standards.

3. If the vehicle or engine cannot be modified to bring it within a class of vehicles or engines represented by a test vehicle or engine for which a certificate of conformity has been issued, the importer or consignee must undertake to demonstrate that the vehicle or engine is in conformity with emission standards by having the vehicle tested in accordance with the regulations of the U.S. Environmental Protection Agency.

Reference 40 C.F.R. §85.1504

11   <u>Admission Pending Receipt of Information.</u> A vehicle or engine imported under a declaration that the importer or consignee does not possess sufficient information to make a knowledgeable declaration may be conditionally admitted into the United States under bond, but will be denied final admission unless the importer or consignee follows these instructions:

1. The importer or consignee must submit to the U.S. Environmental Protection Agency a written request that the vehicle or engine be conditionally admitted pending receipt of information to determine whether the vehicle or engine is covered by a certificate of conformity, or what modifications, if any, are necessary to bring the vehicle into conformity with standards. The written request must:

    a. Identify the place where the vehicle or engine will be stored pending receipt of information. (See storage requirement below.)

    b. Acknowledge responsibility for custody of the vehicle or engine pending receipt of information.

2. The importer or consignee must redeclare the vehicle or engine under the item determined to be appropriate.

Reference: 40 C.F.R. §85.1505

STORAGE REQUIREMENT AND PROHIBITION OF OPERATION OR SALE OF VEHICLES CONDITIONALLY ADMITTED UNDER ITEMS 9, 10, and 11

A vehicle or engine conditionally admitted pending certification, modification, or receipt of information must be stored and may not be operated on the public highways or sold until the vehicle or engine is granted final admission and the bond is released.

A vehicle or engine conditionally admitted shall not be stored on the premises, or subject to access by or control of, any dealer. (NOTE: The importer or consignee may request that this prohibition be waived if modifications of a vehicle or engine to bring it into conformity must be performed by a dealer.)

Failure to comply with these instructions can subject the importer to a fine up to the amount of $10,000 per vehicle or engine.
Reference: 40 C.F.R. §85.205, 85.1508

Completed forms should be sent by the Bureau of Customs to: U.S. Environmental Protection Agency
                                                          Manufacturers Operations Division (EN-340)
                                                           Washington, D.C. 20460

UNITED STATES ENVIRONMENTAL PROTECTION AGENCY
WASHINGTON, D.C. 20460

OFFICE OF
AIR, NOISE AND RADIATION

EPA File # _____

[   ]

[Attn:]

The vehicle described on the attached approved EPA "Test Report Form" has been tested and shown to be in conformity with Federal emission requirements. Therefore, approval is given for release of the EPA obligation on the bond for this vehicle.

We appreciate your cooperation in the enforcement of the joint Customs-EPA regulations.

Very truly yours,

Gerard C. Kraus, Chief
Investigation/Imports Section
Manufacturers Operations Division
(EN-340)

Attachment

cc: Importer

NOTE TO IMPORTER: This is an important document. Please keep a copy with the vehicle registration at all times.

UNITED STATES ENVIRONMENTAL PROTECTION AGENCY
WASHINGTON, D.C. 20460

**OFFICE OF
AIR, NOISE AND RADIATION**

Refer to File #

Dear Importer:

The test results which were submitted for the vehicle described on the attached Test Report Form have been rejected. The reason(s) for rejection are noted below:

1. ____Test results exceed applicable standards.

2. ____Modifications not listed and/or not supported by photographs.

3. ____Original Test Report Form not: __enclosed __signed __notarized __complete.

4. ____Incorrect inertia weight and/or horsepower loading used for test.

5. ____Driver's trace not within specifications.

6. ____Diurnal heat build not within specifications.

7. ____FTP times/mileage not within specifications.

8. ____Vehicle lacks fuel filler neck restrictor or unleaded fuel label.

9. ____Inadequate identifying information on driver's or analyzer trace.

10. ____Calibration curves/documentation insufficient or out-of-date.

11. ____Other_____
_____
_____

The EPA obligation on your bond cannot be released until you demonstrate conformity with Federal emission requirements by submitting proper test results. It is important that you refer to the EPA File Number at the top of this page in any correspondence with this office. If you have any questions please telephone me at (202) 382-2504.

Very truly yours,

Alexander C. Hall
Investigation/Imports Section
Manufacturers Operations Division
(EN-340)

• MERCEDES-BENZ 500 SEL AMG •

CHAPTER
13

BONDING YOUR CAR

A bond is a written obligation made binding by a money forfeit if the conditions of the bond are not met.

The DOT and EPA do permit the conditional importation of nonconforming vehicles. However, to ensure that you bring your vehicle into conformity with all safety and emission regulations, *these agencies require that you post a bond equal to the total value of the vehicle and the import duty.* The bond you post with customs will cover both the EPA and the DOT requirements.

Establishing A Bond

The best and fastest way to post your bond is through your customs house broker, to whom you will give your power of attorney. Never put up cash for your bond, as no interest will be paid and the money can be tied up for several months. Instead, use your assets such as your house, business or other properties as collateral for your bond.

There are other methods of establishing a bond such as using an insurance company authorized to write customs entry bonds or through the U.S. Customs Agency or even by direct cash arrangements with U.S. Customs. However, for ease of time and financial considerations, I think the broker plus collateral make the most sense, and I would avoid the other methods.

Once your vehicle enters the United States under bond to ensure compliance with U.S. pollution and safety standards, you must modify the vehicle to meet those standards and get written releases from both the EPA and the DOT in order to release your bond.

After your car has been modified, your modifier will submit a true and complete statement identifying the modifier, describing the exact nature and extent of the work performed, and certifying that the vehicle or equipment has been brought into conformity. The form used by the DOT is in Appendix 2, and the EPA form is the notarized FTP test results.

The National Highway Traffic Safety Administration will issue an approval letter to the District Director of Customs stating that the condition of the bond has been satisfied. You cannot sell or offer to sell the vehicle until the bond has been released.

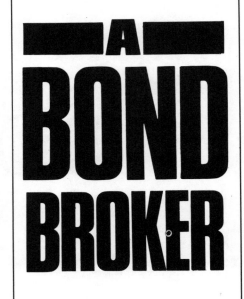

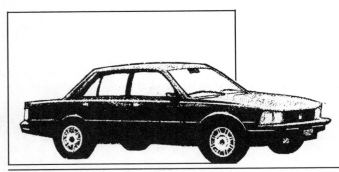

EXTENSIONS

You have 90 days from the date of customs entry to get an EPA release and 120 days from the date of entry to get a DOT release. A DOT extension of 60 days may be granted only by the National Highway Traffic Safety Administration (NHTSA). To apply for this extension, call or write:

Verification Division
Office of Vehicle Safety Compliance
U.S. Department of Transportation,
National Highway Traffic Safety Administration
400 Seventh Street, SW
Room 6113
Washington, DC 20590

Telephone: (202) 426-1693

An EPA extension of the bond must be requested in writing from the customs office (not the EPA) where the vehicle arrived in the United States. You will of course have to provide customs with plausible reasons why you need the extension.

If for whatever reason you are unable to demonstrate your car's conformity with all regulations before the time limits expire, your vehicle will have to be redelivered to customs, exported, or destroyed. Failure to dispose of a nonconforming vehicle by one of these methods will subject you to the assessment of liquidation damages by customs up to the full amount of the bond. In addition, you can be fined. The fines are as much as $10,000 under the Clean Air Act and up to $1,000 per violation, not to exceed $800,000, for any related series of violations. Obviously, this is very serious business, and there is no reason whatsoever to be in this situation.

Whether or not you receive any extensions on your time limits, U.S. Customs will usually wait 180 days before enforcing the law, but don't count on it. Plan on complying with the stated time limits or have the necessary documented extensions. Don't *assume* you have 180 days, because you don't. Do not imagine that they will forget about you if you fail to get your bond released. They *will* come looking for you, and they *will* find and seize your car.

POWER OF ATTORNEY
• PAGE 142

Your customs house broker will provide you with this form which will enable him to release your car without your presence. It should be signed before your car arrives to avoid time lapses causing your car to sit on the docks.

APPLICATION FOR A SECURITY BOND • PAGE 143

This application is available from your customs house broker or directly from U.S. Customs. Apply for your bond several weeks in advance, as it can take anywhere from a few days to weeks to be accepted. Without this bond, your car cannot be released.

POWER OF ATTORNEY

SOCIAL SECURITY # _____

Check appropriate box:

☐ Individual
☐ Partnership
☐ Corporation
☐ Sole Proprietorship

KNOW ALL MEN BY THESE PRESENTS: That, _____

(Full Name of person, partnership, or corporation, or sole proprietorship (Identify))

_____

a corporation doing business under the laws of the State of _____ or a _____

doing business as _____ residing at _____,

having an office and place of business at _____, hereby constitutes and appoints each of the following persons

_____

(Give full name of each agent designated)

as a true and lawful agent and attorney of the grantor named above for and in the name, place, and stead of said grantor from this date and in Customs District_____ and in no other name, to make, endorse, sign, declare, or swear to any entry, withdrawal, declaration, certificate, bill of lading, or other document required by law or regulation in connection with the importation, transportation, or exportation of any merchandise shipped or consigned by or to said grantor; to perform any act or condition which may be required by law or regulation in connection with such merchandise; to receive any merchandise deliverable to said grantor;

To make endorsements on bills of lading conferring authority to make entry and collect drawback, and to make, sign, declare, or swear to any statement, supplemental statement, schedule, supplemental schedule, certificate of delivery, certificate of manufacture, certificate of manufacture and delivery, abstract of manufacturing records, declaration of proprietor on drawback entry, declaration of exporter on drawback entry, or any other affidavit or document which may be required by law or regulation for drawback purposes, regardless of whether such bill of lading, sworn statement, schedule, certificate, abstract, declaration, or other affidavit or document is intended for filing in said district or in any other customs district;

To sign, seal, and deliver for and as the act of said grantor any bond required by law or regulation in connection with the entry or withdrawal of imported merchandise or merchandise exported with or without benefit of drawback, or in connection with the entry, clearance, lading,

unlading or navigation of any vessel or other means of conveyance owned or operated by said grantor, and any and all bonds which may be voluntarily given and accepted under applicable laws and regulations, consignee's and owner's declarations provided for in section 485, Tariff Act of 1930, as amended, or affidavits in connection with the entry of merchandise;

To sign and swear to any document and to perform any act that may be necessary or required by law or regulation in connection with the entering, clearing, lading, unlading, or operation of any vessel or other means of conveyance owned or operated by said grantor;

And generally to transact at the customhouses in said district any and all customs business, including making, signing, and filing of protests under section 514 of the Tariff Act of 1930, in which said grantor is or may be concerned or interested and which may properly be transacted or performed by an agent and attorney, giving to said agent and attorney full power and authority to do anything whatever requisite and necessary to be done in the premises as fully as said grantor could do if present and acting, hereby ratifying and confirming all that the said agent and attorney shall lawfully do by virtue of these presents; the foregoing power of attorney to remain in full force and effect until the _____ day of _____, 19____, or until notice of revocation in writing is duly given to and received by the District Director of Customs of the district aforesaid. If the donor of this power of attorney is a partnership, the said power shall in no case have any force or effect after the expiration of 2 years from the date of its receipt in the office of the district director of customs of the said district.

IN WITNESS WHEREOF, the said _____

has caused these presents to be sealed and signed: (Signature) _____

(Capacity) _____ (Date) _____

WITNESS: _____ _____

(Corporate seal)

CUSTOMS FORM 5291 (10-07-80)

INDIVIDUAL OR PARTNERSHIP CERTIFICATION

CITY _____

COUNTY _____ } ss:

STATE _____

On this _____ day of _____, 19____, personally appeared before me _____

residing at _____, personally known or sufficiently identified to me, who certifies that

_____ (is)(are) the individual(s) who executed the foregoing instrument and acknowledge it to be _____ free act and deed.

_____

(Notary Public)

CORPORATE CERTIFICATION

(To be made by an officer other than the one who executes the power of attorney)

I, _____, certify that I am the _____

of _____, organized under the laws of the State of _____

that _____, who signed this power of attorney on behalf of the donor, is the _____

of said corporation; and that said power of attorney was duly signed, sealed, and attested for and in behalf of said corporation by authority of its governing body as the same appears in a resolution of the Board of Directors passed at a regular meeting held on the _____ day of _____, now in my possession or custody. I further certify that the resolution is in accordance with the articles of incorporation and bylaws of said corporation.

IN WITNESS WHEREOF, I have hereunto set my hand and affixed the seal of said corporation, at the City of _____ this _____ day of _____, 19____.

_____ _____

(Signature) (Date)

If the corporation has no corporate seal, the fact shall be stated, in which case a scroll or adhesive shall appear in the appropriate, designated place.

Customs powers of attorney of residents (including resident corporations) shall be without power of substitution except for the purpose of executing shipper's export declarations. However, a power of attorney executed in favor of a licensed customhouse broker may specify that the power of attorney is granted to the customhouse broker to act through any of its licensed officers or any employee specifically authorized to act for such customhouse broker by power of attorney.

*NOTE: The corporate seal may be omitted. Customs does not require completion of a certification. The grantor has the option of executing the certification or omitting it.

FIREMEN'S INSURANCE COMPANY OF NEWARK. NEW JERSEY
COMMERCIAL INSURANCE COMPANY OF NEWARK, N.J.
NIAGARA FIRE INSURANCE COMPANY
THE FIDELITY AND CASUALTY COMPANY OF NEW YORK
THE BUCKEYE UNION INSURANCE COMPANY

BOSTON OLD COLONY INSURANCE COMPANY
PHOENIX ASSURANCE COMPANY OF NEW YORK
NATIONAL-BEN FRANKLIN INSURANCE COMPANY OF ILLINOIS
NATIONAL-BEN FRANKLIN INSURANCE COMPANY OF MICHIGAN
THE GLENS FALLS INSURANCE COMPANY

APPLICATION FOR A SURETY BOND

Branch Office _____	Bond No. .... ; Form of Bond: ....
Name of Agency	Amount of Bond: $ .... ; Premium: $ .... ;
	Bond to be in force from .... 19 ......
	to .... 19 ......

Application is hereby made to one of the above named Companies (hereinafter called "The Company")

to act as surety on a bond to be given by ....
(Full name of individual, firm or corporation)

....
(Full business address here)

to indemnify ....

to be filed with ....

and to be designated as a .... bond. The bond is to be written in the sum

of $ .... ; is to be dated ...., 19........, and is to be conditioned as follows:

....

1. Nature of Applicant's business: ....
2. Date of beginning business under present individual or firm name: ....
3. Have any claims been made or legal proceedings begun against the Applicant or any member of the firm or corporation in connection with the obligations covered by the bond now applied for? ....
   If so, give particulars. ....
4. Are there any unsatisfied judgments standing against the Applicant? ....
   If so, give particulars: ....
5. Has any company refused to issue or continue a bond for this purpose for the Applicant? ....
   If so, give particulars: ....
6. Names of officers of the Applicant, if a corporation, or of all partners, if a firm: ....

NAME AND TITLE	RESIDENCE
....	....
....	....
....	....
....	....

The corporation was organized in the year .... under the laws of the State of ....

Financial Statement of the Applicant as of .... , 19 ....

Cash on hand:			Due banks within one year:		
Cash in banks:			Names of banks:		
Names of banks:					
			Accounts payable, within one year		
Accounts receivable, current			Notes payable, within one year		
Notes receivable, within one year			Reserve for taxes		
Stocks and Bonds (current market)			Other liabilities payable within one year		
Merchandise inventory					
Total Current Assets			Total Current Liabilities		
Real Estate or Plant, consisting of (give location and description of each parcel):			Mortgages on real estate or plant: (Explain nature and when payable)		
1.			1.		
2.			2.		
3.			3.		
4.			4.		
In whose name is the title?			Other liabilities, consisting of:		
Other assets:			Bank debts payable after one year		
C.S.V. Life insurance			Other debts payable after one year		
Equipment					
			Capital Stock (paid in) if a corporation		
			Surplus and Undivided Profits		
Total Assets,			Total Liabilities:		

STATEMENT OF EARNINGS For period beginning .... , 19 ...... , and ending .... , 19 ....

Sales (Gross revenues) .... $ ....

Net Profit (Before taxes) .... $ ....

Net Profit (After taxes) .... $ ....

[If a full financial statement of recent date (but not otherwise) has been compiled, the Applicant may attach the same to this application, and may complete the following section instead of making up a fresh statement of the form required by section 7.]

8.   A copy of the financial statement of the Applicant dated .... , showing a capital

of $ .... and a surplus of $ .... , is hereto attached and made a part hereof. The said statement is in all respects full, true, and correct.

9.   References as to the record, character, and business standing of the Applicant:

NAME	BUSINESS	POST-OFFICE ADDRESS

The Undersigned further agrees to reimburse and save harmless and indemnify the Company for, from, and against any and all loss, damage, or expense that it shall or may at any time sustain, incur, or become liable for by reason of or on account of its having executed the said bond, or any extension, amendment, or renewal of the said bond, or a new bond as continuation thereof or a substitute therefor or in conjunction therewith; also for, from, and against any and all costs and expenses that may be incurred by the Company in investigating any claim made thereunder, or in or about prosecuting or defending any action, suit or other proceedings that may be commenced or prosecuted by or against the undersigned, his or their heirs, executors, administrators, successors, or assigns, or against the Company, upon the said bond or otherwise in relation thereto. The undersigned hereby consents that any evidence of payment by the Company of any loss, damage or expense sustained by the Company by reason of the execution of the said bond shall, in the absence of fraud on the part of the Company in making such payment, be conclusive evidence against the Undersigned and his or their estate of the fact and extent of the liability of the Company as surety upon the said bond.

In the event the Company executes said bond or other instrument with co-sureties, or reinsures any portion of said bond or other instrument with reinsurers, or procures the execution of such bond or other instrument, the Undersigned further agrees that all of the terms and conditions of this agreement shall apply and operate for the benefit of such other companies, as their interests may appear.

The Undersigned further consents that the Company shall have the right at any time to terminate its future liability as surety on any bond issued by it for the Undersigned on this application and in the event of such action on the part of the Company the Undersigned agrees to furnish the Company with evidence satisfactory to it of the termination of its liability, and agrees that the Company shall not be responsible to the undersigned for any loss or damage that may result to him or them by reason of such action, any statutory provisions to the contrary notwithstanding. The provisions of Section 204.075 Wisconsin Statutes are hereby specifically waived.

Signed, sealed and dated this .... day of .... , 19 ....

IF INDIVIDUAL sign here:

Witness: .... (Seal)

IF COPARTNERSHIP sign here:

Witness: .... (Seal)

.... (Seal)
(Individually and as a copartner)

.... (Seal)
(Individually and as a copartner)

.... (Seal)
(Individually and as a copartner)

IF CORPORATION sign here:

....
(Name of corporation)

(Seal) ....   By ....
                        Secretary   President

ADDITIONAL INDEMNITY

In consideration of THE COMPANY executing or procuring the execution of the bond or bonds herein applied for, including every continuation, renewal, substitute or modification thereof, the undersigned, jointly and severally with the applicant, join in and are bound by the foregoing application and indemnity agreement therein contained in all respects as if the undersigned had executed the same as applicant; the undersigned warranting sufficient interest in the performance of the obligation which the bond or bonds applied for may be given to secure, and assert that the undersigned are fully empowered to be obligated by this agreement.

Signature(s) of Indemnitor(s)

Witness: .... (Seal)

Witness: .... (Seal)

Witness: .... (Seal)

Witness: .... (Seal)

State of ....
                                                                                    } ss:
County of ....

The foregoing indemnity agreement was signed and the signature acknowledged before me, a Notary Public, this ....

day of .... , 19 ....

....
Notary Public

PORSCHE DP 935

CHAPTER
14

UNITED STATES CUSTOMS AND DUTY

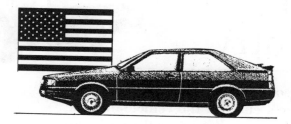

As noted in chapter 6, you will purchase your car duty-free in Europe. However, you will still have to pay duty in the United States. All vehicles of foreign manufacture imported into the United States, whether new or used, whether for personal use or for sale, are subject to duties at the following rates:

- Automobiles: 2.6 percent in 1985 and 2.5 percent in 1986

- Trucks valued at $10,000 or more: 2.5 percent

- Motorcycles up to 700cc: 4.2 percent to 5.5 percent

- Motorcycles over 700cc: Be careful! Motorcycles imported from Japan are subject to duties of up to 49 percent. Contact the nearest customs office for current rates. Rates for motorcycles—even those of less than 700cc—may change drastically. Inform yourself before you buy one, or better yet don't buy one for private importation!

If you purchased the vehicle, and you are not a relative or business associate of the seller, the customs appraised value of the vehicle is normally the price you paid (or agreed to pay) the seller. If the seller received the purchase price in a currency other than U.S. dollars, you must convert the price to U.S. dollars at the rate of exchange on the date your vehicle was exported from the country where you bought it. Exchange rates are available from U.S. Customs. Your customs house broker will pay your fee. If you do not hire a broker, then you will pay the customs duty officer.

If you bought your vehicle from a relative, business associate, or any other seller who is a related party, or if you did not purchase the car (e.g.: it was a gift or you inherited it), the value of the vehicle will be based on the European market. For value information call your local customs office.

CUSTOMS VEHICLE VALUE

Filing Your Customs Entry

As the owner of an imported vehicle you are legally responsible for making a correct entry of the vehicle into the United States. You may authorize a licensed customs house broker to file the entry forms for you. No one other than you or a customs house broker acting for you—even if you give them a power of attorney—may prepare your entry forms. Even customs employees may not prepare your entry papers for you.

So this is another example of why you should hire a customs house broker. Your broker will have posted your bond before you go through customs. Then your customs house broker will file your forms and pay your duty for you. These services are worth their modest fees.

The customs officers who examine your vehicle and documents will determine what kind of entry you must file. In general:

- **If your vehicle is a 1967 or older model, see the inspector at the dock where your car was unloaded. The inspector will collect any duty due and release your car.**

- If your vehicle is a 1968 or newer model, meets U.S. pollution and safety standards, and bears labels placed on the car by the original manufacturer certifying that it meets the standards, see the inspector at the dock where your vehicle was unloaded. The inspector will collect any duty due and release your car.

- If your vehicle is a 1968 or newer model and either does not meet U.S. pollution or safety standards, or lacks the original manufacturer's certifying labels, you may file an informal entry under bond. Once you have a bond, go to the information office for forms and instructions for nonconforming vehicles.

California State Requirements: U.S. Customs does not enforce California smog, vehicle registration, or dealer licensing laws or collect any state sales tax on vehicles. Since any car which is ultimately to be registered in California will eventually have to meet that state's strict requirements, you should call the California Department of Motor Vehicles and find out where you stand.

CUSTOMS AND MODIFICATION REQUIREMENTS

U.S. Customs does not and cannot give any information on the modifications that must be made on your vehicle to comply with EPA and DOT standards. Nor will they advise you on locating a firm to do these modifications.

It is a violation of federal law (19 USC 1592) to give customs officials false or misleading information in order to evade customs duty or to avoid complying with laws or regulations enforced by customs. Penalties for doing so include fines and seizure of the vehicle involved.

Information about customs procedures and documents you must provide to release your vehicle can be found in chapter 9, *Arrival Procedures*. For any other information call your local customs office or write for complete information on importing a car including customs publication number 520.

Department of the Treasury
U.S. Customs Service
Washington, DC 20229

CONSUMPTION ENTRY FORMS • PAGES 150–151 →

This form must be filed when your vehicle enters the United States. Either your customs house broker or you must fill it out (it will be given to you by a customs agent).

CONSUMPTION ENTRY
UNITED STATES CUSTOMS SERVICE

RECORD COPY ☐
CASHIER'S COPY ☐

This Space For Census Use Only			
BLOCK AND FILE NO.	M.O.T.		
	MANIFEST NO.		

Form approved.
O.M.B. No. 48-R0217

This Space For Customs Use Only
ENTRY NO. AND DATE

FOREIGN PORT OF LADING	U.S. PORT OF UNLADING	Dist. and Port Code	Port of Entry Name

Importer of Record (Name and Address)

For Account of (Name and Address)

Importing Vessel (Name) or Carrier	B/L or AWB No.	Port of Lading	I.T. No. and Date
Country of Exportation	Date of Exportation	Type and Date of Invoice	I.T. From (Port)
U.S. Port of Unlading	Date of Importation	Location of Goods—G.O. No.	I.T. Carrier (Delivering)

MARKS & NUMBERS OF PACKAGES COUNTRY OF ORIGIN OF MERCHANDISE (1)	DESCRIPTION OF MERCHANDISE IN TERMS OF T.S.U.S. ANNO., NUMBER AND KIND OF PACKAGES (2)		ENTERED VALUE IN U.S. DOLLARS (3)	T.S.U.S. ANNO. REPORTING NO. (4)	TARIFF OR I.R.C. RATE (5)	DUTY AND I.R. TAX (6)	
	GROSS WEIGHT IN POUNDS (2a)	NET QUANTITY IN T.S. U.S. ANNO. UNITS (2b)				DOLLARS	CENTS

MISSING DOCUMENTS	THIS SPACE FOR CUSTOMS USE ONLY

I declare that I am the ☐ nominal consignee and that the actual owner for customs purposes is as shown above, or ☐ consignee or agent of the consignee. I further declare that the merchandise ☐ was or ☐ was not obtained in pursuance of a purchase or agreement to purchase. I also include in my declaration all the statements in the declaration on the back of this entry.

.... DATE
.... (Signature)
.... (Address)

{
☐ *Principal.*
☐ *Member of the firm,*
.... *of the corporation.*
(Title)
☐ *Authorized agent*
}

CUSTOMS FORM 9-12-73 7501

DECLARATION OF NOMINAL CONSIGNEE, CONSIGNEE, OR AGENT OF CONSIGNEE

To the best of my knowledge and belief, all statements appearing in this entry and in the invoice or invoices and other documents presented herewith and in accordance with which the entry is made, are true and correct in every respect; the entry and invoices set forth the true prices, values, quantities, and all information as required by the laws and the regulations made in pursuance thereof; the invoices and other documents are in the same state as when received; I have not received and do not know of any other invoice, paper, letter, document, or information showing a different currency price, value, quantity, or description of the said merchandise, and if at any time hereafter I discover any information showing a different state of facts I will immediately make the same known to the District Director of Customs at the port of entry.

If the merchandise is entered by means of a seller's or shipper's invoice, no customs invoice for any of the merchandise covered by the said seller's or shipper's invoice can be produced due to causes beyond my control. If the merchandise is entered by means of a statement of the value or the price paid in the form of an invoice, it is because neither seller's, shipper's, nor customs invoice can be produced at this time.

CARRIER'S CERTIFICATE AND RELEASE ORDER

Date ....

The undersigned carrier, to whom or upon whose order the articles described herein or in the attached document must be released, hereby certifies that the consignee named in this document is the owner or consignee of such articles within the purview of section 484(h), Tariff Act of 1930. In accordance with the provisions of section 484(j), Tariff Act of 1930, authority is hereby given to release the articles covered by the aforementioned statement to such consignee.

....
(Name of carrier)

....
(Agent)

AUTHORITY TO MAKE ENTRY FOR PORTION OF CONSOLIDATED SHIPMENT

The merchandise covered by this entry or such portion thereof as may be specifically indicated was shipped by .... consigned to .... endorsed to .... covered by* .... dated .... at .... on file with the district director of customs at ....

I
We } .... the consignee in the above mentioned document covering merchandise for various ultimate consignees, hereby authorize .... or order to make customs entry for the merchandise.

....
(Consignee)

(Transfer of the above authority may be made by endorsement here.)

*Insert "Bill of lading," "Certified duplicate bill of lading," "Carrier's certificate," or "Shipping receipt."

Note:

Term Bond No —If single entry bond is filed insert "S.E."
Importing Vessel or Carrier.—Show the name of vessel or carrier and motive power. If imported by plane or train show also flight or train number.
Type and Date of Invoice.—If entry includes more than one invoice show number of invoices and include information for each invoice in the body of the form in column provided for Description of Merchandise.
Duty and I.R. Tax.—Show separately amount of duty, internal revenue tax, and/or tea inspection fee on each item listed. Internal revenue tax assessments should be preceded by the letters "IR." Tea inspection assessments should be preceded by the letters "TI." If the entry represents more than one dutiable item, the amounts of duty, internal revenue tax, and tea inspection fee should be totaled and labeled separately "Total Duties," "Total I.R. Tax, " and/or "Total T.I. Fee" and recorded together with an aggregate total labeled "Total Collections" in the extreme lower portion of this column.

For information relative to the preparation and filing of a customs entry see UNITED STATES CUSTOMS REGULATIONS and TARIFF SCHEDULES OF THE UNITED STATES ANNOTATED FOR STATISTICAL REPORTING.

BROKER OR AGENT ....
(Name)   (Address)

MERCEDES-BENZ SEL

TAXES:
EUROPEAN
AND
UNITED STATES

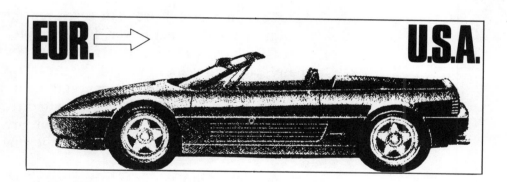

AVOID EUR. V.A.T.

Europe

Two classes of people may avoid paying sales taxes or value added taxes (V.A.T.) in Europe:

- **Those with permanent residence outside the country where the vehicle is purchased (e.g.: tourists, traveling business people).**

- **Those with temporary residence (fewer than two years) in the country where the vehicle is purchased (e.g.: students, temporary workers).**

The avoidance of European taxes represents quite a significant savings to a car buyer. For example, the V.A.T. in West Germany is 14 percent. If you buy your vehicle in Germany, you will get a refund of the tax by presenting the export bill of lading, registration, and your passport to German Customs. Your dealer will have to direct you to the correct customs office since not all of them are authorized to make this refund. Your refund will be made immediately.

If you plan to buy your car by phone, telex, or personal contacts, the value added tax will, upon shipment, have to be cleared by your dealer. Make sure in advance that your dealer will do this, because in essence you never should pay this tax, so be sure your dealer understands that you are aware of this, and you expect him to manage this for you.

United States

When you register your vehicle in your home state, you will have to pay your state's sales or use taxes. It is important for you to contact your state's Department of Motor Vehicles, as some states have exceptions. For example:

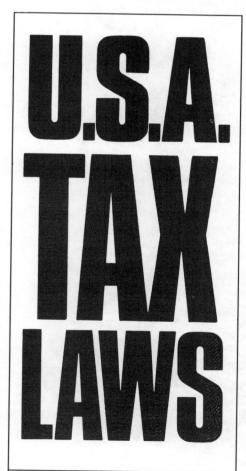

- **In California, prior out-of-state use of the vehicle in excess of 90 days from the date of purchase to the date of entry into California, exclusive of any time of shipment or storage for shipment to California, will be accepted as proof of intent that the vehicle was not purchased for use in California. The period of use for purpose of this 90-day test is measured from the date the purchaser takes possession at the out-of-country point to the time the vehicle is delivered to a shipping agent or placed in storage for shipment to California.** *The state may require proof that you have used the car in Europe or other parts of the United States, so be sure to save all gas and service receipts.*

  If you live outside California, you might check with your state tax office to see if a similar exemption is available to you.

- **In California, vehicles sold by the parent, grandparent, or spouse of the purchaser, or by a brother or sister of the purchaser if both are under the age of 18 and are related by blood or adoption, where the seller is not engaged in the business of selling vehicles, are usually exempt from state sales and use taxes. Claimants of this exemption must submit satisfactory evidence of relationship.**

Sales taxes are the same for new and used cars. Mileage does not affect these taxes. However, the laws vary from state to state. For instance, in Florida you can avoid paying sales taxes on your vehicle if you register it out of the state for six months. In New York you pay sales tax on the car, and if you have owned the car outside the United States for six months, you will pay tax on the fair market value of the car at the time you pay the tax. In Texas everyone pays sales tax, no matter how long the car has been owned.

Not only do the tax laws vary from state to state, they change frequently. Since this book is not intended to be a comprehensive guide in this area, I strongly urge you to check with the tax department in your home state.

YOUR IMPORTATION CALENDAR AND CHECKLIST

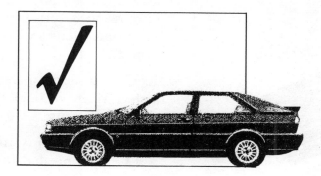

At this point, you know everything involved in importing a European car. You know the processes and procedures necessary to achieve full compliance with all U.S. regulations. I feel, from my own personal experience, that you can give a positive answer to the questions you might have initially asked. Is importation something you can reasonably hope to do? Yes! Is it something you can do profitably? Yes! Is it something you can do in your spare time? Yes! Is it something you can do legally in full compliance with the law? Yes! Can you realize a significant savings? Yes!

An Importation Calendar

Now that you know all about the process of importation, I want to be absolutely certain that you do not encounter any delays along the way, which could prove costly, aggravating and disappointing.

Timing is an important element in a smooth car importation. Mostly, this means having the right papers in hand and having made complete prior arrangements well in advance of each stage of importation.

Overall, the whole process from making your deposit with a European dealer to completion of all modifications and acceptance of all paperwork by the EPA and DOT, to finally driving your dream car will vary according to your personal plans. But once you have selected your car and it is ready to ship to the United States, it will take only five or six weeks from European shipment to receiving state plates from the Department of Motor Vehicles (add an extra week for shipment to the West Coast).

But let's take a closer look at what you should do, starting with writing to possible European dealerships.

- Initial letters of inquiry to reputable European dealers. Please note that Europeans conduct business on a very formal level, and any communications should respect this polite formality.

- Decision to buy a particular vehicle from a dealer. Write to dealer and check on the following points:

    - Available inventory
    - Time needed for special features you are ordering
    - Confirm cost
    - Check on dealer's willingness to supply you with *international transit plates, registration, insurance*, as well as having European use taxes and value added taxes refunded
    - Be sure your dealer will also handle shipping arrangements and marine insurance

- Receive satisfactory confirmation from dealer.

- Select your conversion center and discuss the feasibility and cost of converting your car. This is especially important to do *before buying your car* if you will be buying a special or exotic car. Be sure to check the credentials and references of your conversion center.

- Contact your bank and inform them of what you are doing. Arrange to have a deposit sent to your European dealer, and establish an international letter of credit or other secure form of financing your car.

- Contact your customs house broker, and advise as to what you are doing. If you will be traveling in Europe, you'll want to keep your customs house broker abreast of your plans so he can act on your behalf. Set the customs house broker up with your power of attorney so he can pick up the ball while you are away, and alert him as to your shipper, your conversion center, and your insurance carrier.

- Confirm with your conversion center the kind of car and the date and place of its arrival in the United States.

- Check on all of your insurance coverage. Remember you need:
    - *Travel insurance* if you are traveling (your European dealership should set this up). This should be B and E, the best possible insurance you can get. Be sure it covers your entire stay in Europe, and confirm the dates on your green insurance card. Remember no insurance, no registration, no driving in Europe.
    - *Marine Insurance:* Your dealer or shipper should set this up but check for *complete reliable coverage* with a reputable insurer.
    - *Stateside Coverage:* Be sure your car is covered from the moment it arrives, through conversion process and registration, when your private car insurance program will kick in.

- Always keep track of your registration card in the *original*. Never give it to anyone. This is a critical paper and it is costly to replace.

Files

I suggest that you keep very careful records of all communications concerning your importation. Of course, you will keep all official forms and letters of agreement, but also jot down dates and content of phone conversations, as well as to whom you were speaking. The more complete your records, the less apt you will be to overlook any critical details.

EUROPEAN FILE

- Your dealership's name, address, phone and telex number, as well as the salesperson's name who is handling your importation.
- All receipts
- Registration card certificate in the original
- Green insurance card
- Customs documents, if any, such as Spanish bail bond
- Shipping and marine insurance file
- Bill of sale
- Tax refunds

U.S. CUSTOMS FILE

- Customs house broker—name, address, telephone
- Customs forms from broker
- Power of attorney
- Pick-up order
- Bond application
- Receipts

DOT

EPA

DMV

DOT FILE

- Conversion center—name, address, telephone, name of contact and copy of agreement
- Form HS-189 (statement of compliance)
- P.C.I. assignment
- DOT letter of approval (or)
- DOT letter of rejection
- Receipts

EPA FILE

- EPA waiver (if applicable)
- EPA declaration Form 3520-1
- F.T.P. test results
- F.T.P. test reports
- EPA letter of approval (or)
- EPA letter of rejection
- Receipts

Department of Motor Vehicles

As every state varies in what it needs, keep all insurance and registration papers, as well as any tax and mileage verification papers.

Selecting Reliable People and Companies

It should not be necessary for you to personally go through all the steps involved in the importation of a car. Other people will do most of these things for you. I have detailed all of the steps involved so you will be aware of what others are doing. I think you should know as much about the process of importing, converting, and certifying a car as the people who will be doing all the legwork for you. If you know all that is involved, you will not be completely at the mercy of people who have more knowledge than you. Also, you can check on their progress to make sure they are doing all you are paying for, doing it correctly, and doing it on time. By understanding the process of importing a car, you will be better able to hire the right people to help you.

To profitably import an automobile from Europe without having the project take over your life, you will need the help of four parties:

- An honest *European dealer* experienced in sales to individuals buying vehicles for export to the United States

- A reliable *shipping company*

- A reliable *customs house broker*

- An honest, experienced *conversion center*

These people and companies will do most of the work for you. If you understand what they will be doing—and you should, now that you have finished this book—you should merely have to keep tabs on their progress to make sure that everything is done correctly.

BROKER

CONVERSION CENTER

Your *European dealer* will sell you a car. He will arrange for your temporary registration if you plan to drive the car in Europe. He will arrange to have European use taxes and value added taxes refunded to you. Your dealer will also arrange to insure your car if you plan to drive it in Europe. He will make shipping arrangements as well as marine insurance arrangements if you so request. If the person who wants to sell you a car is not prepared to do these things for you, go somewhere else. Dealers experienced in selling to Americans fully expect to provide all these services.

Your *shipping company* will in many cases pick up your car in any major city in Europe. They will help you arrange marine insurance. They will steam clean your car's undercarriage. They will take care of all the paperwork involved in exporting your car.

When your vehicle arrives in the United States, your *customs house broker* will continue the process. He will pay terminal clearance charges, arrange customs clearances, pay the duty, and arrange for the issuance of a bond.

When the customs house has finished its work, your *conversion center* will step in. The conversion center will pick up your car at the docks. They will bring it into line with all DOT and EPA safety and emission regulations. They will take the car to the testing lab and will complete all the paperwork involved in getting your car approved for use on U.S. roads.

If you take this approach to importing a car—that is, if you hire competent, experienced people to handle all the details while you oversee their work—you *can* import a fine European automobile in your spare time, and you *can* save a significant amount of money doing it. Not only will you have an interesting and stimulating experience, but you will find yourself the owner of a fine car—in some cases a rare, exotic car—for far, far less than any of your neighbors have paid.

The keys to entering the American gray market are knowledge and the desire to save money. After reading this book, you should have both those keys. Put them to work opening doors for you now!

Trip Checklist

If you are traveling abroad and plan on picking your car up, driving it through Europe, and then shipping it home, there are a few additional reminders. Remember, you want to avoid any delays because your car should be something that enhances your travel rather than taking up your valuable leisure time.

I strongly recommend that you order your vehicle in advance of your trip. Leaving for Europe with the idea that you will "find" a car once you arrive unfortunately can be very disappointing. There are often limited inventories, and you simply may not be able to get your dream car. I urge you to make all of your plans, negotiate your arrangements with your European dealer, make your deposit, and do as much on the Importation Calendar as possible before you leave.

This way, you'll be free to pick up your car, make your final payment, and drive off to enjoy your vacation.

Here are a few reminders that will save you time, help in your planning, and avoid any disappointment.

- **Be sure you contact a reputable conversion center in advance of your trip. Give them the approximate date for the arrival of your car. They should advise you of their procedures and suggest a customs house broker.**

- **Before you leave, contact the customs house broker and write down any of their requirements and specific procedures.**

- **Keep your stateside insurance agency well-informed of your plans. Tell them the model and make of the car you are importing, as well as the approximate arrival date. They will open a file. Call them from Europe to confirm your purchase and the arrival date for your car. This way, your car will be covered the moment it arrives in the United States.**

- **Be sure your car will always be insured: policy to cover European travel (arranged by dealer), marine insurance for shipping (arranged by dealer or shipper), and stateside insurance upon arrival (arranged by you).**

- Get an international driver's license issued by major AAA offices throughout the United States. If there will be more than one driver in your group, be sure each one has an international driver's license.

- Before you leave the United States, alert your European dealer to your need for international transit plates, registration and insurance for driving in Europe. Check your registration carefully, and also check cancellation date on your green insurance card. Also let your dealer know when you will arrive, so that all paperwork will be ready. This way you simply have to pay the balance, and drive your car away.

- Confirm with your dealer that he has made arrangements for shipment and marine insurance. Confirm the dates and ports in advance.

- Acquire maps of the countries you plan to visit and plan your itinerary. Be sure to include some translation books.

- Don't forget your address book, and a complete file of your car importation transactions (photocopy the papers you do not need in the original while in Europe).

- Buy traveler's checks in U.S. dollars, but also in foreign currencies for emergency use. This is especially important to avoid problems with money when you have late evening arrivals, or travel on weekends and holidays.

- Make sure that all papers including the important registration and bill of lading (B/L) *are under your name.*

- As I mentioned earlier, do not send your car under consolidation. Be sure your name alone is on the bill of lading as importer.

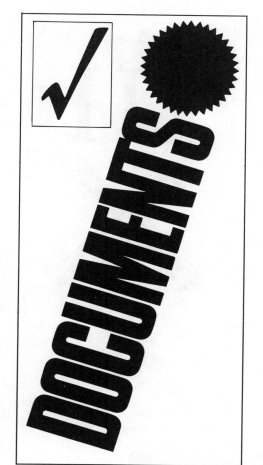

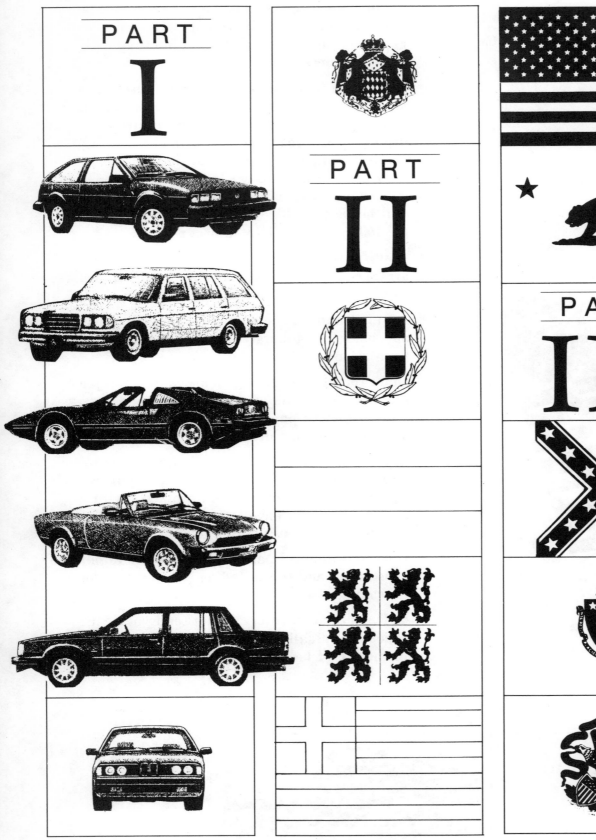

PART I

PART II

PART III

APPENDICES

APPENDIX
1

SUMMARY DESCRIPTION OF DOT STANDARDS

PAGES 169 TO 177

→

Here are very explicit descriptions of all DOT standards applicable to passenger cars, campers, trucks, buses and motorcycles. The importance for you as a private importer is that you grasp the overall scope of requirements. Of course, many European cars already conform to many of these standards. Your conversion center knows exactly which areas need modification to fully comply with the law.

SUMMARY DESCRIPTION OF DOT STANDARDS[*]

STANDARD NO. 101 – Controls and Displays
Passenger Cars (Effective 1-1-68):

Requires that essential controls be located within reach of the driver when the driver is restrained by a lap belt and upper torso restraint, and that certain controls mounted on the instrument panel be identified.

Passenger Cars (Effective 1-1-72), Multipurpose Passenger Vehicles, Trucks, and Buses (Effective 9-1-72):

All manually operated controls must be identified by words.

Passenger Cars, Multipurpose Passenger Vehicles, Trucks, and Buses (Effective 9-1-72):

Except for foot-operated controls or manually operated controls mounted on the steering column, the identification of essential controls and displays must be illuminated whenever the headlamps are lit.

Passenger Cars, Multipurpose Passenger Vehicles, Trucks, and Buses (Effective 9-1-80):

Certain essential hand-operated controls and certain displays must be identified by symbol, and such identification be illuminated.

STANDARD NO. 102 – Transmission Shift Lever Sequence, Starter Interlock, and Transmission Braking Effect
Passenger Cars, Multipurpose Passenger Vehicles, Trucks, and Buses (Effective 1-1-68):

Requires that the automatic transmission shift lever sequences have the neutral position placed between forward and reverse drive positions. Its purpose is to reduce the likelihood of driver error in shifting. Also required is an interlock to prevent starting the vehicle in reverse and forward drive positions and an engine-braking effect in one of the lower gears at vehicle speeds below 25 miles per hour.

STANDARD NO. 103 – Windshield Defrosting and Defogging Systems
Passenger Cars, Multipurpose Passenger Vehicles, Trucks, and Buses (Effective 1-1-68):

Requires that all vehicles manufactured for sale in the continental United States be equipped with windshield defrosters and defogging systems. Test conditions are also specified for passenger cars.

---

[*] Title 49 Code of Federal Regulations Part 571.

STANDARD NO. 104 – Windshield Wiping and Defrosting Systems

Passenger Cars (Effective 1-1-68), Multipurpose Passenger Vehicles, Trucks, and Buses (Effective 1-1-69):

Specifies the windshield area to be wiped and requires high-performance washers with two or more speed power-driven systems. The wipers must be able to sweep the windshield at least 45 times a minute, regardless of engine load. Tables prescribing the minimum size of wiped areas have been added for passenger cars.

STANDARD NO. 105 – Hydraulic Brake System

Passenger Cars (Effective 1-1-68), and School Buses (Effective 4-1-77), Other Buses, Trucks and Multipurpose Passenger Vehicles (Effective 9-1-83):

Requires motor vehicles utilizing hydraulic brakes to have a split brake system, incorporating service and emergency features that are capable of stopping the vehicle under certain specified conditions, a parking brake system capable of holding light vehicles on a 30 per cent grade and heavy vehicles on a 20 per cent grade, and a warning light system to indicate loss of pressure or low fluid level, antilock system failure, and parking brake application.

STANDARD NO. 106 – Brake Hoses

Passenger Cars and Multipurpose Passenger Vehicles (Effective 1-1-68), Trucks, Buses, Trailers, Motorcycles, and Equipment (Effective 9-1-74):

The standard establishes performance and labeling requirements for hydraulic, air, and vacuum brake hoses, brake hose assemblies, and brake hose fittings for all motor vehicles.

STANDARD NO. 107 – Reflecting Surfaces

Passenger Cars, Multipurpose Passenger Vehicles, Trucks, and Buses (Effective 1-1-68):

The reflection of the sun into the driver's eyes from shiny surfaces has long been a safety hazard. This standard requires that windshield wiper arms, inside windshield moldings, horn rings, and frames and brackets of inside rearview mirrors have matte surfaces which will greatly reduce the likelihood of hazardous reflection into the driver's eyes.

STANDARD NO. 108 – Lamps, Reflective Devices, and Associated Equipment

Passenger Cars, Multipurpose Passenger Vehicles, Trucks, Trailers, Buses, and Motorcycles (Effective 1-1-68 for vehicles 80 or more inches in width, effective 1-1-69 for all others):

This standard specifies requirements for lamps, reflective devices, and associated equipment for signaling and to enable safe operation in darkness and other conditions of reduced visibility. Side marker lights and reflectors, hazard warning and backup lights, and replacement equipment are included in the requirements for these vehicles.

STANDARD NO. 109 - New Pneumatic Tires
Passenger Cars (Effective 1-1-68):

Specifies tire dimensions and laboratory test requirements for bead unseating resistance; strength, endurance, and high-speed performance; defines tire load rating; and specifies labeling requirements.

STANDARD NO. 110 - Tire Selection and Rims
Passenger Cars (Effective 4-1-68):

Specifies requirements for original equipment tire and rim selection on new cars to prevent overloading. These include placard requirements relating to load distribution as well as rim performance requirements under conditions of tire deflation.

STANDARD NO. 111 - Rearview Mirrors
Passenger Cars, Multipurpose Passenger Vehicles (Effective 1-1-68), Trucks, Buses, and Motorcycles (Effective 2-26-77):

Specifies requirements for rearview mirrors to provide the driver with a clear and reasonably unobstructed view of the rear. On passenger cars it requires an outside rearview mirror on the driver's side, and when the inside mirror does not provide a sufficient field of view because of the size or location of the rear window, an additional outside mirror on the passenger side is required. Also, the inside mirror must be designed to reduce the likelihood of injury on impact. Trucks and buses must have mirrors on both sides.

STANDARD NO. 112 - Headlamp Concealment Devices
Passenger Cars, Multipurpose Passenger Vehicles, Trucks, Buses, and Motorcycles (Effective 1-1-69):

Specifies that any fully opened headlamp concealment device shall remain fully opened whether either or both of the following occur: (a) any loss of power to or within the device, or (b) any malfunction of wiring or electrical supply for controlling the concealment device.

STANDARD NO. 113 - Hood Latch Systems
Passenger Cars, Multipurpose Passenger Vehicles, Trucks, and Buses (Effective 1-1-69):

Specifies requirements for a hood latch system for each hood. A front-opening hood which in any open position partially or completely obstructs a diver's forward view through the windshield must be provided with a second latch position on the hood latch system or with a second hood latch system.

STANDARD NO. 114 - Theft Protection
Passenger Cars (Effective 1-1-70):

This standard requires that each passenger car have a key-locking system that whenever the key is removed prevents normal activation of the car's engine and also prevents either steering or self-mobility of the car, or both.

STANDARD NO. 115 - Vehicle Identification Number
Passenger Cars (Effective 1-1-69), Multipurpose Passenger
Vehicles, Trucks, Buses, and Trailers (Effective 9-1-80):
> Specifies requirements for the content and format of a
> number to facilitate identification of a vehicle and must be
> permanently affixed to the vehicle.

STANDARD NO. 116 - Hydraulic Brake Fluids
(Effective 1-1-68, Amended 3-1-72):
> Requires minimum physical characteristics for three grades
> of brake fluids, DOT 3, DOT 4, and DOT 5, for use in hydrau-
> lic brake systems in all motor vehicles. Also establishes
> labeling requirements for brake fluid and hydraulic system
> mineral oil.

STANDARD NO. 117 - Retreaded Pneumatic Tires
Passenger Cars (Effective 1-1-72):
> Prohibits certain practices in manufacture of retreaded
> tires which might weaken the completed tire. Certain label-
> ing information is also required.

STANDARD NO. 118 - Power-Operated Window Systems
Passenger Cars and Multipurpose Passenger Vehicles
(Effective 2-1-71):
> This standard specifies requirements to minimize the likeli-
> hood of death or injury from accidental operation of power-
> operated window systems. Requires that power-operated win-
> dow systems be inoperable when ignition is in an off posi-
> tion or when key is removed.

STANDARD NO. 119 - New Pneumatic Tires
Multipurpose Passenger Vehicles, Trucks, Buses, Trailers, and
Motorcycles (Effective 3-1-75):
> Specifies strength, endurance, and high speed performance
> and marking requirements for new pneumatic tires manufac-
> tured for use on multipurpose passenger vehicles, trucks,
> trailers, buses, and motorcycles.

STANDARD NO. 120 - Tire Selection and Rims
Vehicles Other Than Passenger Cars (Effective 8-1-76):
> This standard requires new vehicles to have tires conforming
> to Standard No. 119 or Standard No. 109 and rims designated
> in the tire association manuals as fitting them. It speci-
> fies marking requirements for rims and requires additional
> tire and rim size designations, pressure and speed restric-
> tions, and weight rating information.

STANDARD NO. 121 - Air Brake Systems
Trucks, Buses (Effective 3-1-75), and Trailers
(Effective 1-1-75):
> Establishes performance and equipment requirements on vehi-
> cles equipped with air brake systems, for service, emergen-
> cy, and parking brake capability.

STANDARD NO. 122 - Motorcycle Brake Systems
Motorcycles (Effective 1-1-74):
> Establishes equipment and performance requirements on brake systems appropriate for two-wheeled and three-wheeled motor-cycles. Each motorcycle is required to have either a split hydraulic service brake system or two independently actuated service brake systems.

STANDARD NO. 123 - Motorcycle Controls and Displays
(Effective 9-1-74):
> Specifies requirements for the location, operation, identi-fication and illumination of motorcycle controls and dis-plays and for stands and footrests.

STANDARD NO. 124 - Accelerator Control Systems
Passenger Cars, Multipurpose Passenger Vehicles, Trucks, and Buses (Effective 9-1-73):
> Establishes requirements for the return of a vehicle's throttle to the idle position when the driver removes his or her foot from the accelerator control, or in the event of a breakage or disconnection in the accelerator control system.

STANDARD NO. 125 - Warning Devices (Effective 1-1-74):
> Establishes shape, size, and performance requirements for reusable day and night warning devices that can be erected on or near the roadway to warn approaching motorists of the presence of a stopped vehicle. It applies only to devices that do not have self-contained energy sources.

STANDARD NO. 126 - Truck-Camper Loading (Effective 1-1-73):
> Requires manufacturers of slide-in campers to affix a label to each camper that contains information relating to certi-fication, identification, and proper loading and to provide more detailed loading information in the owner's manual.

STANDARD NO. 201 - Occupant Protection in Interior Impact
Passenger Cars (Effective 1-1-68), Multipurpose Passenger Vehicles, Trucks, and Buses (9-1-81) 10,000 lbs. or less:
> Over a wide range of impact speeds, injuries suffered by occupants are largely determined by how well the structures on the inside of the vehicle cushion the human body hitting them. This standard specifies requirements to afford impact protection for occupants. It contains requirements for padded instrument panels, seat backs, sun visors, armrests. Glove compartment doors are required to remain closed during a crash.

STANDARD NO. 202 - Head Restraints
Passenger Cars (Effective 1-1-69):
> Specifies requirements for head restraints to reduce the frequency and severity of neck injuries in rear-end and other collisions.

STANDARD NO. 203 – Impact Protection for the Driver From the Steering Control System

Passenger Cars (Effective 1-1-68), Multipurpose Vehicles, Trucks, and Buses GVWR [Gross Vehicle Weight Rating] of 10,000 lbs. or less (Effective 9-1-81):

Specifies requirements for minimizing chest, neck, and facial injuries by providing steering systems that yield forward, cushioning much of his or her impact energy in front-end crashes. Such systems are highly effective in reducing the likelihood of serious and fatal injuries.

STANDARD NO. 204 – Steering Control Rearward Displacement

Passenger Cars (Effective 1-1-68), Multipurpose Passenger Vehicles, Trucks, and Buses with Unloaded Vehicle Weight of 4,000 Pounds or less (Effective 9-1-81):

Specifies requirements limiting the rearward displacement of the steering column into the passenger compartment to reduce the likelihood of chest, neck, or head injuries.

STANDARD NO. 205 – Glazing Materials

Passenger Cars, Multipurpose Passenger Vehicles, Trucks, and Buses (Effective 1-1-68):

Specifies requirements for all glazing materials used in windshields, windows, and interior partitions of motor vehicles. Its purpose is to reduce the likelihood of lacerations and to minimize the possibility of occupants penetrating the windshield in collisions.

STANDARD NO. 206 – Door Locks and Door Retention Components

Passenger Cars (Effective 1-1-68), Multipurpose Passenger Vehicles (Effective 1-1-70), and Trucks (Effective 1-1-72):

Requires locking systems and specifies load requirements for door latches and door hinge systems to minimize the probability of occupants being thrown from the vehicle as a result of forces encountered in vehicle impact.

STANDARD NO. 207 – Seating Systems

Passenger Cars (Effective 1-1-68), Multipurpose Passenger Vehicles, Trucks, and Buses (Effective 1-1-72):

Establishes requirements for seats, their attachment assemblies, and their installation, to minimize the possibility of failure as a result of forces acting on the seat in vehicle impact.

STANDARD NO. 208 – Occupant Crash Protection

(Effective 3-10-71):

This standard specifies requirements for both active and passive occupant crash protection systems for passenger cars, multipurpose passenger vehicles, trucks, and the driver's seat in buses. Generally the following options are permitted:

Passenger Cars (Effective 1-1-68):

Lap or lap and shoulder seat belt assemblies in each designated seating position; except in convertibles, lap and shoulder seat belts are required in each front outboard seating position.

Passenger Cars (Effective 1-1-72):
(a) A complete passive protection system, or
(b) Lap belts with belt warning and meeting certain crash protection requirements specified for a 30-mph frontal barrier crash, or
(c) In each designated seating position a lap or lap and shoulder seat belt assembly with seat belt warning; seat belt assemblies in outboard designated seating positions must have a single-point pushbutton release and emergency-locking or automatic-locking seat belt retractors.

Passenger Cars (Effective 9-1-73):
Same requirements as for passenger cars effective 1-1-72 except that the upper torso restraints must adjust by means of an emergency-locking retractor.

Buses (Effective 1-1-72):
The bus driver's seat must be equipped as follows:
(a) A complete passive protection system or
(b) A lap or lap and shoulder seat belt assembly.

Multipurpose Passenger Vehicles and Trucks (Effective 1-1-72):
Certain multipurpose passenger vehicles and trucks must meet option "a" or option "b" specified for passenger cars, above.

STANDARD NO. 209 – Seat Belt Assemblies
Passenger Cars, Multipurpose Passenger Vehciles, Trucks, and Buses (Effective 3-1-67):
   Specifies requirements for seat belt assemblies. The requirements apply to straps, webbing, or similar material, as well as to all necessary buckles and other fasteners and all hardware designed for installing the assembly in a motor vehicle, and to the installation, usage, and maintenance instructions for the assembly.

STANDARD NO. 210 – Seat Belt Assembly Anchorages
Passenger Cars (Effective 1-1-68), Multipurpose Passenger Vehicles, Trucks, and Buses (Effective 7-1-71):
   Specifies the requirements for seat belt assembly anchorages to ensure effective occupant restraint and to reduce the likelihood of failure in collisions.

STANDARD NO. 211 – Wheel Nuts, Wheel Discs, and Hub Caps
Passenger Cars and Multipurpose Passenger Vehicles and Equipment (Effective 1-1-68):
   Requires that "spinner" hub caps and other winged projections (both functional and nonfunctional) be removed from wheel nuts, wheel discs, and hub caps. Its purpose is to eliminate a potential hazard to pedestrians and cyclists.

STANDARD NO. 212 - Windshield Mounting

Passenger Cars (Effective 1-1-70), Multipurpose Passenger Vehicles, Trucks, and Buses 10,000 lbs. or Less (Effective 9-1-78):

This standard requires that, when tested as described, each windshield mounting must be anchored in place and retain one of two specified percentages of its periphery in a crash situation. The purpose of the standard is to keep vehicle occupants within the confines of the passenger compartment during a crash.

STANDARD NO. 213 - Child Seating Systems

(Effective 4-1-71, amended 1-1-81):

Specifies requirements for dynamic testing of child seating systems to minimize the likelihood of injury and/or death to children in vehicle crashes or sudden stops. Includes requirements for providing information for proper installation and use.

STANDARD NO. 214 - Side Door Strength

Passenger Cars (Effective 1-1-73):

This standard specifies requirements for crush resistance levels in side doors of passenger cars to minimize the safety hazard caused by intrusion into the passenger compartment in a side impact accident.

STANDARD NO. 215

[Superseded by PART 581 on 9-1-78.]

STANDARD NO. 216 - Roof Crush Resistance

Passenger Cars (Effective 9-1-73):

Sets minimum strength requirements for passenger car roofs to reduce the likelihood of roof collapse in a rollover accident. The standard provides an alternative to conformity with the rollover tests of Standard No. 208.

STANDARD NO. 219 - Windshield Zone Intrusion

Passenger Cars (Effective 9-1-76), Multipurpose Passenger Vehicles, Trailers, Buses of 10,000 lbs. or Less GVWR (Effective 9-1-77):

The purpose of this standard is to reduce crash injuries and fatalities that result from occupants contacting vehicle components displaced near or through the windshield. The standard regulates the intrusion of parts from outside the occupant compartment into a defined zone in front of the windshield during a frontal barrier crash test.

STANDARD NO. 301 - Fuel System Integrity

Passenger Cars (Effective 1-1-68), Multipurpose Passenger Vehicles, Trucks, and Buses Under 10,000 lbs (Effective 9-1-76), and School Buses Over 10,000 lbs. (Effective 4-1-77):

This standard specifies requirements for the integrity and security of the entire fuel system, including the fuel tanks, fuel pump, carburetor, emission controls, lines, and connections in severe front, rear, or lateral barrier impact crash tests. Manufacturers must also be able to demonstrate

that fuel loss will not exceed one ounce per minute in a
static rollover test following these barrier crash tests, as
well as not exceeding these limits after, and incidental to,
the crash tests.

STANDARD NO. 302 – Flammability of Interior Materials
Passenger Cars, Multipurpose Passenger Vehicles, Trucks, and
Buses (Effective 9-1-72):
This standard specifies burn resistance requirements for
materials used in the occupant compartment of motor vehicles
in order to reduce deaths and injuries caused by vehicle
fires.

SUMMARY DESCRIPTION OF OTHER REGULATIONS

PART 555 – Temporary Exemptions from Motor Vehicle Safety Standards (Effective 1-29-73):
This regulation provides a means by which manufacturers of
motor vehicles may obtain temporary exemptions from specific
safety standards on the grounds of substantial economic
hardship, facilitation of the development of new motor vehicle safety or low-emission engine features, or existence of
an equivalent overall level of motor vehicle safety.

PART 580 – Odometer Disclosure Requirements (Effective 9-30-78):
The regulation requires a person who transfers ownership of
a motor vehicle to give the transferee a written disclosure
of the mileage the vehicle has traveled.

PART 581 – Bumper Standard
Limited Damage (Effective 9-1-78); No Damage (Effective 9-1-79):
This standard specifies limitations on damage to non-safety-
related components and vehicle surface areas. It also in-
corporates the requirements previously contained in Safety
Standard No. 215.
Vehicles manufactured after September 1, 1978, must also be
certified as conforming to the bumper standard required by
the Cost Savings Act. This requirement has been incorporated into 49 CFR 567.

APPENDIX
2

DOT
FORM HS-189

PAGES 179 TO 182

→

This important DOT form will be filled out along with the picture book by your conversion center. You will enter the P.C.I. number on Page 1 of the form and sign as importer. Send the complete form to the address at the top of the form.

DEPARTMENT OF TRANSPORTATION
NATIONAL HIGHWAY TRAFFIC SAFETY ADMINISTRATION
DIRECTOR, OFFICE OF VEHICLE SAFETY COMPLIANCE (NEF-32) (CUS)
400 7th STREET, SW
WASHINGTON, D.C. 20590
(Complete this form and mail to above address)

Form Approved

O.M.B. No. 2127-0012

STATEMENT OF COMPLIANCE

"This is to Certify that the motor vehicle described below conforms to all applicable Federal Motor Vehicle Safety Standards (FMVSS) in effect on the date of manufacture, as indicated below."

Name of Importer as shown on Customs Entry *(Type or Print)*	Port of Entry	Customs Entry Number and Date
Make and Model of Vehicle		Year Manufactured
Complete Chassis Serial Number *(Include all Prefixes)*	Engine Serial Number	
Please Sign Here — Signature of Importer	PCI Number	Date

Please Note:

You must indicate on the line next to each requirement outlined below the status of compliance, i.e., indicate:

ORIGINAL _____ If the item was part of the original factory equipment;

MODIFIED O/S _____ If the modification was made overseas;

MODIFIED IN USA _____ If the modification was made in USA subsequent to importation.

You *must* attach to this Statement of Compliance all vouchers and receipted work orders identifying the modifier and describing the *exact* nature and extent of work performed.

The Applicability Key is as follows:

PC = Passenger Car
MPV = Multi-Purpose Passenger Vehicle

TRK = Truck
BUS = Bus

The numerals 1–68, etc., indicate that the requirement is applicable to vehicles manufactured on or after January 1, 1968, etc.

All subsequent pages and attached vouchers and documents must show the importer's name and vehicle chassis serial number.

The listing shown below is not intended to represent the complete or detailed requirements of the Federal Motor Vehicle Safety Standards, but only to indicate the areas of apparent noncompliance which may exist with respect to your vehicle.

Indicate if item is Original, Modified O/S or Modified in USA

FMVSS 101

CONTROL LOCATION, IDENTIFICATION, AND ILLUMINATION

This part applies to: PC = 1–68

The following controls, when mounted on the instrument panel, must be identified:

Headlamps

Choke (if manual)

Windshield defrosting and defogging system

Windshield wiping system

Windshield washing system

This part applies to: PC = 1–72 MPV = 9–72 TRK = 9–72 BUS = 9–72

All manually-operated controls must be identified as follows:

Word or Abbreviation	Permissible Symbol
CHOKE	None
THROTTLE	None
LIGHTS	⬡
HAZARD	⚠
CLEARANCE LAMPS or CL LPS	☀
IDENTIFICATION LAMPS or ID LPS	None
WIPER or WIPE	▽
WASHER or WASH	⊛
DEFROST or DEF	None

Indicate if item is Original, Modified
O/S or Modified in USA

FMVSS 108

LAMPS, REFLECTIVE DEVICES, AND ASSOCIATED EQUIPMENT

This part applies as follows:

Vehicles of 80 or more inches overall width:
PC=n/a MPV=1-68 TRK=1-68 BUS=1-68 TRL=1-68

Vehicles regardless of width:
PC=1-69 MPV=1-69 TRK=1-69 BUS=1-69 TRL=1-69

The vehicle must be equipped with the following components:

_____ Two 7″ or four 5″ sealed beam headlamp units

_____ Two red tail lamps and two red stop lamps (amber stop lamps may be used on vehicles manufactured prior to 1-72)

_____ One white license plate lamp   *_____ Must have a three lamp ID cluster front & rear TRK rear TRL

_____ Two Class-A reflectors on rear of vehicle *_____ Must have clearance lamps

_____ One white backup lamp

_____ Turn signal lamps *(two red or amber lamps on rear of vehicle, and two amber lamps on front)*

_____ Four-way flasher hazard warning system

_____ Two amber or white parking lamps on front *(applies only to vehicles less than 80″ overall width)*; effective 1-70, parking lamps must be on when headlamps are on.

Side markers:
_____ One red reflector and one red lamp on each side at rear *(one red reflector or one red lamp may be used on vehicles manufactured prior to 1-70).*

_____ One amber reflector and one amber lamp on each side at front *(one amber reflector or one amber lamp may be used on vehicles manufactured prior to 1-70).*

FMVSS 109

NEW PNEUMATIC TIRES

This part applies to: PC=1-68 MPV=n/a TRK=n/a BUS=n/a

_____ The symbol "DOT" and manufacturer's name or assigned code number must be molded into the tire.

Tires manufactured after May 21, 1971 must have a tire identification number molded into the tire in the space directly above, below, or to the left or right of the symbol "DOT".

COPY THE INFORMATION APPEARING ON EACH TIRE, RELATING TO THE ABOVE, IN THE SPACES BELOW:

FMVSS 110

TIRE SELECTION AND RIMS

This part applies to: PC=4-68 MPV=n/a TRK=n/a BUS=n/a

A placard must be affixed to the glove compartment door or an equally accessible location, displaying the following:

_____ Vehicle capacity weight *(rated cargo and luggage load plus 150 pounds times the vehicle's designated seating capacity).*

_____ Designated seating capacity *(expressed in terms of total number of occupants and in terms of occupants for each seat location).*

_____ Vehicle manufacturer's recommended cold tire inflation pressure for maximum loaded vehicle weight.

_____ Vehicle manufacturer's recommended tire size designation.

COPY THE VALUES SHOWN ON THE PLACARD IN THE SPACE BELOW:

Vehicle capacity weight _____   Designated seating capacity _____

Manufacturer's recommended
cold tire inflation pressure   FRONT: _____ psi   REAR: _____ psi

Manufacturer's recommended
tire size designation   FRONT: _____   REAR: _____

Printed name of importer   Complete chassis serial number

FMVSS 121

AIR BRAKE SYSTEMS

This part applies to MPV=3-1-75 TRK=3-1-75 BUS=3-1-75 TRL=3-1-75
Each vehicle must have, among other things, a service brake
system acting on all wheels. (Effective 7-24-80)

FMVSS 124

ACCELERATOR CONTROL SYSTEMS

This part applies to: PC=9-73 MPV=9-73 TRK=9-73 BUS=9-73

The accelerator control system must have at least two sources of energy capable of returning the throttle to the idle position within one second from any accelerator position whenever the driver removes the opposing actuating force.

In the event of failure of one source of energy by a single severance or disconnection, the throttle arm shall return to the idle position within one second from any accelerator position or speed whenever the driver removes the opposing actuating force.

The throttle shall return to the idle position from any speed of which the engine is capable whenever any one component of the accelerator control system is disconnected or severed at a single point. The return to idle shall occur within one second from the time of severance or disconnection or from the first removal of the opposing actuating force by the driver.

FMVSS 201

OCCUPANT PROTECTION IN INTERIOR IMPACT

This part applies to: PC=1-68 MPV=n/a TRK=n/a BUS=n/a

The following components must afford impact protection for occupants which is equal to that provided on model certified by the manufacturer:

Instrument panel

Seat backs

Sun visors *(two are required)*

Armrests

Interior compartment doors *(effective 1-70)*

FMVSS 202

HEAD RESTRAINTS

This part applies to: PC=1-69 MPV=n/a TRK=n/a BUS=n/a

The vehicle must be equipped with head restraints at each outboard front designated seating position to withstand a rearward test load of 200 pounds at a point 2½ inches below the top of the head restraint or 25 inches above the seating reference point *(the approximate position of the human torso and thigh)*. The top of the head restraint shall be not less than 27½ inches above the seating reference point.

FMVSS 203

IMPACT PROTECTION FOR THE DRIVER FROM STEERING CONTROL SYSTEM

This part applies to: PC=1-68 MPV=9-81 TRK=9-81 BUS=9-81

The vehicle must be equipped with steering control components, including the steering wheel, which are equal to those installed on model certified by the manufacturer. There shall be no components or attachments, including horn actuating mechanisms and trim hardware, which can catch on the driver's clothing or jewelry *(watches, rings, and bracelets without loosely attached or dangling members)*.

FMVSS 204

STEERING CONTROL REARWARD DISPLACEMENT

This part applies to: PC=1-68 MPV=9-81 TRK=9-81 BUS=9-81

The vehicle must be equipped with a steering control system which will assure that the upper end of the steering column and shaft will not be displaced in a rearward direction by more than 5 inches when the vehicle is subjected to a barrier collision test at 30 miles per hour.

FMVSS 205

GLAZING MATERIALS

This part applies to: PC=1-68 MPV=1-68 TRK=1-68 BUS=1-68

AS-1 specification and the manufacturer's distinctive designation or trademark must be etched on the windshield.

AS-1 or AS-2 specification and the manufacturer's distinctive designation or trademark must be etched on all other window glass.

Effective 4-73, each piece of glazing material must additionally bear the symbol "DOT" and the manufacturer's code mark assigned to him by NHTSA.

COPY THE MARKINGS SHOWN ON THE WINDSHIELD AND WINDOWS IN THEIR ENTIRETY IN THE SPACE BELOW:

Printed name of importer	**Complete chassis serial number**

FMVSS 209

_____

SEAT BELT ASSEMBLIES

This part applies to: PC=1-68 MPV=1-68 TRK=1-68 BUS=1-68

Each seat belt assembly shall be permanently and legibly marked or labeled with year of manufacture, model, and name or trademark of manufacturer or distributor, or importer if manufactured outside the United States.

All seat belt assemblies shall be accompanied by written instructions for the proper use of the assembly.

Copy the markings shown on the seat belt assemblies in their entirety in the space below.

FMVSS 210

_____

SEAT BELT ASSEMBLY ANCHORAGES

This part applies to: PC=1-68 MPV=1-68 TRK=1-68 BUS=1-68

Seat belt anchorages shall be installed for each designated seating position for which a seat belt assembly is required.

FMVSS 211

_____

WHEEL NUTS, WHEEL DISCS, AND HUB CAPS

This part applies to: PC=1-68 MPV=1-68 TRK=n/a BUS=n/a

Wheel nuts, hub caps, and wheel discs for use on passenger vehicles shall not incorporate winged projections.

FMVSS 212

_____

WINDSHIELD MOUNTING

This part applies to: PC=1-70 MPV=*9-78 TRK=*9-78 BUS=*9-78

The windshield must be mounted in such way as to equal, in parts and installation procedure, the mounting in a model certified by the manufacturer, such mounting to retain not less than 75% of the windshield periphery when the vehicle is subjected to a barrier collision test at 30 miles per hour.

* Gross vehicle weight ratings of 10,000 lbs or less

FMVSS 214

_____

SIDE DOOR STRENGTH

This part applies to: PC=1-73 MPV=n/a TRK=n/a BUS=n/a

Any side door in the vehicle that can be used for occupant egress shall have a peak crush resistance of not less than two times the curb weight of the vehicle or 7,000 pounds, whichever is less.

FMVSS 215
PART 581

_____

_____

_____

EXTERIOR PROTECTION

This part applies to: PC=9-72 MPV=n/a TRK=n/a BUS=n/a

The exterior protection components, including bumpers, must prevent low-speed collisions from impairing the safe operation of vehicle systems, and to reduce the frequency of override or underride in higher speed collisions when:

The vehicle impacts a fixed collision barrier while traveling forward at 2-1/2 mph.

The vehicle impacts a fixed collision barrier while traveling rearward at 2½ mph.

This part applies to: PC=9-73 MPV=n/a TRK=n/a BUS=n/a

The vehicle's front surface and rear surface is impacted three times each with a pendulum test device equal in mass to the test vehicle and moving at 2½ mph. _(The pendulum requirement does not apply to a vehicle manufactured prior to 9-74 that has a wheelbase of 115 inches and that either has a convertible top; has no roof support structure between the A-pillar and the rear roof support structure; or has no designated seating position behind the front designated seating position.)_

This part applies to: PC=9-75 MPV=n/a TRK=n/a BUS=n/a

In addition to the above, the vehicle's front and rear corners are impacted once each with a pendulum test device equal in mass to the test vehicle and moving at 1½ mph.

Printed name of importer	Complete chassis serial number

3

SAFETY COMPLIANCE INFORMATION SHEET

PAGES 184 TO 185

→

This form will help you understand the safety compliance regulations of the DOT.

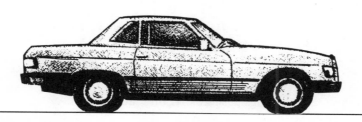

SAFETY COMPLIANCE INFORMATION SHEET

This information is furnished to assist you in correcting safety deficiencies that your vehicle may have, and guide you in your preparation of your compliance statement so that your bond may be released.

Please note that while your vehicle may have some of the required safety features, there are areas where compliance with the given Federal Motor Vehicle Safety Standards (FMVSS) is questionable. Unless you clearly substantiate conformity of your vehicle with all applicable FMVSS, including those questionable where modifications may not have been required, your statement may appear unclear and be rejected until you submit additional data. In such cases the bond release action is delayed due to additional correspondence involved.

To simplify the aspect of technical substantiation of your vehicle's compliance, we suggest that you use photographs showing the respective safety feature which you describe in the written part of your statement; this is in addition to the "Statement of Compliance", Form HS-189. Where photographs cannot be made or would be impractical to use, furnish a detailed description of the item so that there is no question of compliance and/or your understanding of the requirement. Examples of statements substantiating compliance are shown below and on the reverse side hereof. However, these are not all-inclusive and do not represent the requirements of all FMVSS that may apply to your vehicle.

Remember that:
a. All items on the vouchers identify the FMVSS to which they apply otherwise it may be impossible to recognize them as pertinent to the issue.
b. Photographs must be clear to be of value and identify the FMVSS features which are referenced in the written part of the statement of compliance.
c. All individual pages, photographs, vouchers, sheets of paper, etc, must show the full and correct chassis serial number of the vehicle to which they apply to prevent loss or misplacement.
d. Your statement of compliance must be signed and dated. If the importer of record, as shown on the Form HS-7 and the FMVSS printout, is a company, there must be enclosed a notarized statement (use of corporate seal is acceptable) by an recognized officer of the company designating a person authorized to sign the statement of compliance in behalf of the company. Statements bearing an unidentified signature will be rejected.
e. While there may be requirements which, in your opinion, are unnecessary, there is no provision in the law under which anyone may be exempted from compliance.

Listed below are some of the FMVSS where compliance is questionable in vehicles which were not manufactured for the U.S. market. You should therefore describe how your vehicle meets these requirements even if modifications were not required, providing that the given FMVSS is applicable to your vehicle as shown on the printout already furnished to you. When filling out the Form HS-189, write "N/A" where the requirement is not applicable.

FMVSS
101 - Control identification by word/symbol
      Illumination of control identification
102 - Shift pattern on gearshift knob or elsewhere
105 - Dual circuit brake master cylinder
      Brake failure warning system, including warning
      lamp and means for testing it
108 - Sealed beam headlamps; parking lamps; sidemarker
      lamps and reflectors
110 - Tire information placard
111 - Outside mirror within reach of driver
114 - Steering lock; ignition key buzzer
115 - VIN plate on dashboard, nonremovable
202 - Head restraints (headrests)
203 - Impact-absorbing steering wheel
204 - Impact-absorbing steering column

FMVSS
205 - Windshield etched with marking "AS-1"
206 - Rear door locks without possibility to open door from
      inside with door handle when the lock button is down
207 - Front seat backrests with lock (2-door models only)
208 - Seat belts in front and rear; single-point pushbutton
      release; locking retractors; warning light and buzzer
211 - Racing-type wheel nuts with projecting wings
212 - Non-popout windshield (glued-in)
214 - Side door beams (in all dors)
215 - U.S.-type bumpers with additional buffers and cushions
      (9-72 to 8-73); with shockabsorbers, meeting the 5 mph
      impact requirement front and rear (9-73 to 8-78); non-
      damage bumpers, soft-surface, etc (from 9-78 on)
302 - Flammability of interior materials (may be ok if vinyl
      or leather, questionable if cloth)

(*)-Continued below-

EXAMPLES OF SUBSTANTIATING STATEMENTS

Shown below are several examples of statements which may aid you in formulating your own substantiation of compliance:

FMVSS 101 - ORIGINAL: Refer to photograph # ___ showing that all controls subject to this FMVSS are properly identified.

ORIGINAL: Refer to photograph # ___ showing lamp fixtures which illuminate the control identification features subject to this FMVSS. Identification of the following controls is self-illuminated by light sources contained within the fixture itself: (list the controls)

ORIGINAL: Intensity of control illumination is regulated by adjusting the headlamp switch knob.

OR ---

-Continued on other side-

(*)
    Part 581 - Nonconforming bumpers front and rear

FMVSS 101 - MODIFIED: Refer to photograph # __ showing that all controls subject to this FMVSS are properly identified. The only modification required was the installation of a headlamp switch identification plate listed on repair voucher # __, item # __.

MODIFIED: Refer to photograph # __ showing lamps which illuminate the control identification features subject to this FMVSS. The installed lamps are listed on repair voucher # __, item # __.

ORIGINAL: Intensity of control illumination is regulated by the headlamp switch knob (photograph # __). No modifications were required to comply with this part of the standard.

FMVSS 105 - ORIGINAL: Refer to photograph # __ showing the dual brake master cylinder and connecting wires which activate the brake failure warning lamp in the event of failure in the hydraulic brake system. The brake failure warning lamp is located on the dashboard (photograph # __) and its bulb can be tested by actuating the parking brake lever. No modifications were required to meet the requirements of this FMVSS.

OR ---

FMVSS 105 - MODIFIED: Refer to photograph # __ showing the dual brake master cylinder and connecting wires which activate the brake failure warning lamp in the even of failure in the hydraulic brake system (refer to voucher # __, item # __, listing the required brake master cylinder). Refer to photograph # __ showing the brake failure warning lamp as installed on the dashboard (refer to voucher # __, item # __, listing the required lamp). The bulb in the brake failure lamp can be tested by depressing the lamp lens. I performed the modification myself in accordance with instructions contained in the shop manual for this vehicle.

FMVSS 110 - MODIFIED: Refer to photograph # __ showing the required placard as installed in the glove compartment of the vehicle. I purchased the placard from my local dealer.

OR --

FMVSS 110 - MODIFIED: Refer to photograph # __ showing the required placard as installed in the glove compartment of the vehicle. I made the placard myself. I calculated the vehicle capacity weight in the following way:

    Manufacturer's specified maximum permissible gross vehicle weight ...... 4,500 lbs
    Curb weight (car empty with full tank and otherwise road-ready) .... 3,670 lbs
    Vehicle capacity weight (payload) .... 830 lbs

---

FMVSS 212 - ORIGINAL: Refer to statement from the U.S. representative of the manufacturer of this car showing that the windshield is installed in same way as in the U.S.-model of this car. (Statements from sources other than the manufacturer of the vehicle or his U.S. representative are not acceptable because compliance with FMVSS 212 cannot be determined without access to factory records.)

OR ---

FMVSS 212 - MODIFIED: Refer to voucher # __ showing installation of the windshield according to the vehicle manufacturer's specifications, including the use of U.S.-type windshield moulding and special retaining cement.

FMVSS 214 - ORIGINAL: Refer to photograph # __ showing the U.S.-model doors with the reinforcing side beams exposed to view as installed in this vehicle, and copy of page # __ from the vehicle's spare parts manual showing that identical doors are used by the manufacturer in both U.S. and non-U.S. versions of this vehicle.
OR ---

FMVSS 214 - MODIFIED: Refer to photograph # __ showing the modified doors with the reinforcing side beams exposed to view as installed in this vehicle. Also refer to voucher # __, item # __, and to the enclosed engineering analysis showing full formulas and numerical calculations that were used in designing the reinforcements to meet the requirements of this FMVSS.

FMVSS 215 - MODIFIED: Refer to photographs # __ and # __ showing the modified front and rear bumpers, and a copy of page # __ and page # __ from the vehicle's spare parts manual showing all components of U.S.-model front and rear bumpers used to meet the requirements of this FMVSS and installed in this vehicle. The bumpers now represent a copy of those used in the U.S.-model version of this vehicle.

OR ---

FMVSS 215 - MODIFIED: Refer to photographs # __ and # __ showing the modified front and rear bumpers, and to voucher # __, items # __, with enclosed engineering analysis showing full formulas and numerical calculations that were used in designing the reinforced bumper system to meet the requirements of this FMVSS. Photographs # __ thru # __ further illsutrate the bumper and frame reinforcement features.

FEDERAL EMISSION STANDARDS FOR LIGHT-DUTY VEHICLES (EPA)

PAGE 187 →

Upon request, the EPA will send this technical form for emission requirements.

Federal Emission Standards for Light-Duty Vehicles
(Expressed as grams per mile (gpm) and grams per test (gpt))

1970 – 1983 Model Year Vehicles

	1970	1971	1972	1973-1974	1975-1976	1977	1978-1979	1980	1981-1983
HC	4.1 gpm	4.1 gpm	3.0 gpm	3.0 gpm	1.5 gpm	1.5 gpm	1.5 gpm	.41 gpm	.41 gpm
CO	34 gpm	34 gpm	28 gpm	28 gpm	15 gpm	15 gpm	15 gpm	7.0 gpm	3.4 gpm
NOx	N. R.	N. R.	N. R.	3.1 gpm	3.1 gpm	2.0 gpm	2.0 gpm	2.0 gpm	1.0 gpm
Evap.	N. R.	6 gpt	2 gpt	2 gpt	2 gpt	2 gpt	6.0 gpt (SHED)*	6.0 gpt (SHED)*	2.0 gpt (SHED)*

Diesel Particulates	0.60 gpm** (82 and later)

HC = Hydrocarbons   NOx = Oxides of Nitrogen   N. R. = Not Required
CO = Carbon Monoxide   Evap.= Evaporative Hydrocarbons

1968 – 1969 Model Year Vehicles***

141 CID and Greater

Inertia Weight Class		1500	1750	2000	2250	2500	2750	3000	3500	4000	4500	5000	5500	6000
Auto Trans	HC	2.7	3.2	3.7	4.1	4.5	4.9	5.3	5.9	6.5	7.0	7.4	7.7	7.9
Auto Trans	CO	22	26	30	33	37	40	43	48	53	57	60	62	64
Manual Trans	HC	2.5	2.9	3.3	3.7	4.1	4.4	4.7	5.3	5.8	6.3	6.6	6.9	7.1
Manual Trans	CO	20	24	27	30	33	36	39	43	48	51	54	56	57

101 CID to 140 CID

		1500	1750	2000	2250	2500	2750	3000	3500	4000	4500	5000	5500	6000
Auto Trans	HC	3.5	4.1	4.7	5.2	5.8	6.2	6.7	7.6	8.3	8.9	9.4	9.8	10.0
Auto Trans	CO	30	35	40	45	49	53	57	64	70	76	80	83	85
Manual Trans	HC	3.1	3.7	4.2	4.7	5.2	5.6	6.0	6.8	7.4	8.0	8.4	8.8	9.0
Manual Trans	CO	27	31	36	40	44	48	51	58	62	68	72	75	77

50 CID to 100 CID

		1500	1750	2000	2250	2500	2750	3000	3500	4000	4500	5000	5500	6000
Auto Trans	HC	4.1	4.8	5.5	6.1	6.7	7.3	7.9	8.8	9.7	10.4	11.0	11.4	11.7
Auto Trans	CO	34	40	46	51	56	61	66	74	81	87	92	95	98
Manual Trans	HC	3.7	4.3	4.9	5.5	6.1	6.6	7.1	7.9	8.7	9.4	9.9	10.3	10.5
Manual Trans	CO	31	36	41	46	51	55	59	66	73	78	83	86	88

All 1968 and later model year gasoline-fueled vehicles must be equipped with a closed crankcase system.
Evaporative emission testing is not required on diesel-fueled vehicles.

* Evaporative emission testing for 1978 and later model year vehicles must be done according to the SHED procedure.

** Particulate standard applies only to 1982 and later model year diesel-fueled vehicles.

*** 1968 and 1969 model year vehicles not subject to NOx and evaporative standards.

APPENDIX
5

IMPORT CERTIFICATION LABORATORIES FORM (EPA)

PAGE 189

→

This is the form your conversion center will receive showing the vehicle's EPA test results. A copy will be given to you by the conversion center upon request.

IMPORT CERTIFICATION
LABORATORIES

DATE	11-26-84	ENG FAM	N/A	CURB WT	3550
DRIVER	MH	CID	N/A	INERTIA	4000
TEST #	R-1865	TRANS	AUTO	ARHP	13.2
TEST SEQ	CVS II	CARB	FI	IRHP	10.1
VEHICLE	MB2	CAT	YES	FUEL	1HO
MODEL	500 SEC	A/C	YES	DYNO	1
YEAR	1381	ODO	021155	EAC	1
VIN		TECHN	BB	CVS #	1
START TIME	1748	END TIME	1832		
COMMENTS . . .		# 7144	BB		

COLD TRANSIENT

CVS TEMP	113.5						
CVS REVS	12371	VMIX	3146.024	ROLL CTS	8385	MILES	3.5962
TEMP ADB	76	TEMP AWB	56	REL HUM	25.1	BARO	30.10
DELTA P	29.0	INLET P	15.3	NOX CF	.8354	Vo	.28542

AMBIENT BAG		SAMPLE BAG		MASS DATA	
HC PPM	5.7	HC PPM	93.6	HC GRAMS	4.551
CO PPM	5.8	CO PPM	172.699	CO GRAMS	17.384
NOX PPM	.2	NOX PPM	35	NOX GRAMS	4.957
CO2 %	.039	CO2 %	1.594	CO2 GRAMS	2544.231

COLD STABILIZED

CVS TEMP	113.3						
CVS REVS	21261	VMIX	5410.562	ROLL CTS	9021	MILES	3.869
TEMP ADB	75	TEMP AWB	56	REL HUM	27.2	BARO	30.11
DELTA P	29.0	INLET P	15.5	NOX CF	.8406	Vo	.28542

AMBIENT BAG		SAMPLE BAG		MASS DATA	
HC PPM	5.6	HC PPM	11	HC GRAMS	.512
CO PPM	5.906	CO PPM	9.607	CO GRAMS	.735
NOX PPM	.5	NOX PPM	11.1	NOX GRAMS	2.62
CO2 %	.047	CO2 %	.953	CO2 GRAMS	2551.069

HOT TRANSIENT

CVS TEMP	113.7						
CVS REVS	12373	VMIX	3146.522	ROLL CTS	8378	MILES	3.5932
TEMP ADB	75	TEMP AWB	55	REL HUM	24.1	BARO	30.11
DELTA P	29.0	INLET P	15.5	NOX CF	.8276	Vo	.28542

AMBIENT BAG		SAMPLE BAG		MASS DATA	
HC PPM	4.8	HC PPM	20.1	HC GRAMS	.81
CO PPM	6.781	CO PPM	43.326	CO GRAMS	3.858
NOX PPM	.9	NOX PPM	26.6	NOX GRAMS	3.637
CO2 %	.047	CO2 %	1.272	CO2 GRAMS	2005.868

WEIGHTED MASS EMISSIONS SUMMARY

HYDROCARBONS GMS/MI	CARBON MONOZIDE GMS/MI	OXIDES OF NITROGEN GMS/MI	CARBON DIOXIDE GMS/MI
.393	1.395	.914	641.568

URBAN CYCLE FUEL ECONOMY
13.754   MILES PER GALLON

6

MOTOR VEHICLE EMISSION TEST REPORT FORM (EPA)

PAGE 191 ⟶

This form will be filled out by the test lab and sent to the EPA, along with the necessary EPA photos.

MOTOR VEHICLE EMISSION TEST REPORT FORM

Form Approved
OMB No. 2000-0228
Exp. 05/31/85

> **WARNING:** Any person who knowingly makes a false statement on this form is in violation of Federal law and may be fined not more than $10,000 or imprisoned not more than five years, or both. 18 USC 1001.

The Following Items Are To Be Filled In By Importer (Or Consignee) From EPA Form 3520-1

Name and Address of Importer (Or Consignee)	
	Port of Entry
	Date of Entry
	Customs Entry No.

The Following Items Are To Be Filled In By Test Laboratory

Name of Test Laboratory	Address of Test Laboratory		Date of Test
Make of Vehicle	Model of Vehicle	Model Year of Vehicle	Mileage at Time of Test
Vehicle or Chassis Identification No.		Engine Serial No.	Vehicle Curb Weight
Test Procedure		Inertia Weight Class	Transmission Type Auto/Manual
Equipped with PCV System Yes/No	Equipped with Air Conditioning Yes/No	Equipped with Fuel Filler Neck Restrictor Yes/No	"Unleaded Fuel Only" Labels Installed Yes/No
Description of Emission Control Modifications		Photographs of Modifications Enclosed Yes/No	Modifications Performed by:

TEST RESULTS		ALTERNATIVE STANDARDS (See Chart on Back)
HC =	GPM	
CO =	GPM	
NOx =	GPM	
Evap =	GPT	
Part =	GPM	

GPM = Grams per Mile

GPT = Grams per Test

I CERTIFY THAT THE ABOVE VEHICLE HAS BEEN TESTED IN ACCORDANCE WITH TEST PROCEDURES OUTLINED IN 40 CFR 85.075-9 THROUGH 28 (FOR 1968 THROUGH 1977 MODELS) OR 40 CFR, PART 86 (FOR 1978 AND LATER MODELS) AND THAT THE ITEMS FILLED IN BY THE TEST LABORATORY AND THE OFFICIAL FEDERAL TEST PROCEDURE RESULTS SHOWN ABOVE ARE CORRECT.

_____
Signature of Corporate Officer

Subscribed and Sworn To Before Me
This_____Day of_____ 19_____

Notary Public
My Commission Expires:_____

Rev. 8/82 - Previous edition obsolete

WILLIAMSON PUBLISHING CO.

BOX 185, CHURCH HILL ROAD,
CHARLOTTE, VERMONT 05445